HEARD IN OUR LAND

Eugene F. Roop

faithQuest
Elgin, Illinois

Heard In Our Land
Eugene F. Roop

Copyright © 1991 by Eugene F. Roop

faithQuest, a division of Brethren Press, 1451 Dundee Avenue, Elgin, Illinois 60120

Cover design by Jeane Healy

Library of Congress Cataloging-in-Publication Data

Roop, Eugene F.
    Heard in our land/Eugene F. Roop
        p.   cm.
    ISBN 0-87178-351-7
    1. Prayers and meditations. 2. Bible.–Devotional use. I. Title
    BV4532.2.M14 242   91-25132

                                    CIP

Manufactured in the United States of America

Contents

Preface

It is not an act of pride, but of foolishness that allows me to publish these prayers. The prayers arose out of my study for seminary teaching and were shared in connection with various class discussions and lectures. It is dangerous enough to take them out of one context, the classroom, and put them in another, the wider church. But in addition, they are moving from oral literature to written, and from mostly private to public. The courage that enabled such a move belongs not primarily to me, but to the students who asked, cajoled, and sometimes threatened.

I am quite aware that not every student who heard these prayers wanted them printed. Just as no one kind of music gives song to our faith, no one style of prayer gives voice to the soul. It will be a plus if the prayers of this book enable a few, who felt their own prayers too odd or awkward, to risk a bit more in public. I will count it worthwhile if, because of this book, some who felt silenced by a customary style for prayer, will venture their own words. Some may laugh during your prayer, which means they have joined you; or laugh at your prayer, which is painful. Both have happened to me.

Most important for me has been the role of the Bible as the creative energy behind my prayers. To be sure, studying the Bible is my vocation, a context few will duplicate, and most would not want to. Hence for my life of prayer I must thank that Book and the One whose Spirit generated it. I now understand one way in which God prays for me when I have no words, no energy. Beyond the obvious oddity of thanking a Book for this book, I want to thank the students who joined me in prayer, especially Kevin Daggett and Karen Peterson Miller who read, corrected, and pushed this project forward. It is to all students of Bethany Theological Seminary that this book is dedicated.

Gene Roop
June, 1991

Heard in Our Land

The poignant prayers from the Nazi prison by Dietrich Bonhoeffer have reminded us again that prayer erupts from the soul as each individual or community travels through life. Prayer, no matter how mysterious it might seem, happens automatically as the faithful engage in conversation within their own soul or the community of faith. By the time the prayer has been organized enough to reach acceptable oral speech, it may already have lost some of its power. For what to us sounds like prayer has often been filtered through layers of convention that veil the meaning and civilize the rough edges.

That filtering seems to be much less the case in the Bible. Whether it be the prayer of Jesus from the cross or some of the Psalms, which we seldom use because of their rage, to our biblical ancestors, whatever was experienced in life belonged in prayer. Fortunately, as Karl Barth notes in his book *Prayer*, the Protestant reformers entertained no distinction between explicit prayer (that which passes the lips as oral speech) and implicit prayer (that which remains as sentiments of the soul). Even if we are reluctant to go public with our prayer, our silence speaks for us, our soul will not be denied.

Besides the public and private experiences of life, yet another factor has energized the prayers in this book, study of the Bible. Some experience a basic antagonism between biblical study and prayer. Perhaps one can connect prayer with Bible reading or meditation, but not with disciplined, academic study. We have been taught that academic study happens as an act of the mind, and thus such study must be dispassionate and objective. Prayer, on the other hand, comes as the voice of the soul. Its words explode with passion and engage the center of each subject. Conventional wisdom suggests that the two, study and prayer, cannot be merged let alone be interchanged. Academic study lacks interest in matters of the Spirit; prayer does not care about footnotes.

Conventional wisdom has a point, of course, but more needs to be said. A biblical perspective on the person suggests that we must not, and probably cannot, divide the individual in half as conventional wisdom often assumes. We act most fully human when we bring our whole being to any activity. In fact we are probably fooling ourselves if we think we can engage in emotionless research or mindless prayer. My study comes alive if I allow prayer to give voice to the emotions that arise in my work. My prayer is more whole when I allow my mind an equal partnership.

Most of you who read and use these prayers will move in the opposite direction from the process that generated the prayers. You will read the prayer first and then perhaps turn to the biblical text that accompanies each. The prayer may help you see something new in the biblical text. Maybe you will only find confusion, wondering how I got to that prayer from that text. Hopefully such wonder will cause you to study the biblical text on your own and you will find the result stirring deep in your soul.

I suspect more of you will use the prayers to give voice to your own thoughts, expression to your own emotions, quite apart from the biblical text that generated the prayer in my life. In that case, please know that the emotions and thoughts of your soul stir in the heart of the Bible as well. As Hannah and David, Mary Magdalene and Peter discovered, God will receive all that stirs in our soul, the joy and the despair, the love and the hate. Like the sound of the turtledove, whatever is heard in our land, we can find in the Bible and include in our prayer.

Ordinary Days

Focus text: *There is a season for everything, and a time for every event under heaven.*

— Qoheleth, Ecclesiastes 3:1

Most of our lives consist of ordinary days. There may be some people who experience "unusual" adventure everyday. Certainly many people try to create excitement or crisis constantly. However most of us settle into a daily pattern that makes our diary fairly routine.

The old wisdom poem in Ecclesiastes 3 recognizes the ebb and flow of ordinary days, as life moves from birth to death, from planting to harvest, from tears to laughter. Most of us experience genuine satisfaction in being a part of the rhythm of life, even if we do not have much to say when another person asks what we have been doing lately. It means that for the most part our life could not be filmed on location and sold as a television series, whether as a situation comedy or an action packed adventure. Even though we like to watch comedy and adventure on television, we prefer to rest while we do it. It makes me tired just to imagine a life in constant motion whether that motion be fun or frustrating.

Most of our days are spent with ordinary people, the ones we see at home, at work, at church, in the apartment building or neighborhood. We take for granted they will be there. Of course we remember and talk about the celebrities we meet or wish to meet. We recognize their faces in the newspaper and we might catch glimpses of them in an airport. Even celebrities need ordinary friends, not just people who recognize them and point. We need people we can take for granted, those who know us inside as well as by sight. Fortunately for most of us, life is full of ordinary people.

The prayer of blessing and thanks at mealtime recognizes that everyday life and ordinary people belong to God. Very often children and adults repeat the same prayer at each meal, varying the prayer only when guests are present. This prayer may be a common one learned from tradition, or their own prayer, first spoken at some now long forgotten moment. Admittedly this routine prayer may cause us to avoid really recognizing God's presence in our everyday life and prevent us from noticing the unusual things that do happen. Yet this routine prayer can acknowledge that most of life is "normal" and perhaps it is so with God as well.

Much of the Bible is about the extra-ordinary, the "memorable." But hidden between those memorable incidents and extra-ordinary events lies the every-day life of the people. The early church passed on to us the special days of Jesus' life, the days of ecstasy and tragedy. We can safely assume from the myriad of days that were not recorded that most of his life was normal. Clearly Jesus understood that normal days belong in everyday prayer: "Give us each day our daily bread."

An Ordinary Day

I Kings 22:41-53, Matthew 6:25-34

God, what does one say about an ordinary day.
    No crisis, for now, just regular problems and possibilities.

Thank you, God, for an ordinary day,
    Not just ordinary things in the day,
        An ordinary day.
    The wind is calm, relatively,
        And so are we, mostly.
    The traffic moves as planned, for the most part,
        And so do we, usually.

    Of course we could dredge up a lot of problems,
            Most of them clear candidates for the confessional.

    Oppression and violence supported by our tax dollars;
            An economic system that lets some live in the
            streets,
                Building others' homes in Ginger Creek.
    People disabled and hidden from sight;
            A way of relating that looks askance at people
            different,
                Making friends only of those just like us.

    We find little new in that confession,
            And not much spirit in it either.
                Yes, there should be,
                    But we confess, Lord, there isn't.

Thank you, God, that we don't have to be dramatic to be happy,
        We don't require a crisis to know we live.

    Be with those who create problems to get attention,
        Only then does anyone know their name.

    Help us to touch someone who is not crying,
        To stop a moment with someone who is "just fine."

We pray in the name of the one
    who lived most of his life without drama,
        a lot of ordinary days,
            Jesus Christ our Lord. Amen.

Cloudy, Cool Friday

Genesis 26:26-33 , Numbers 35:1-8

God, the city is awake now,
> but a quick look makes it unclear that we are.
>> Oh well, what can we expect on Friday,
>>> And a cloudy, cool Friday at that.

We do expect a lot of ourselves, Lord,
> And we expect some from you as well.

> We expect that we will always be charming and witty,
>> And we expect you to save us from our tendency to say something stupid.
> We expect to always be brilliant and creative,
>> And we expect you to protect us from making any public blunder.
> We expect to always be strong and sensitive with other people,
>> And we expect you to provide us with a constant stream of significant relationships.

God, cast our boring minutes from the calendar.
> Make all our seconds exciting.
>> Wipe away all public blunders,
>>> Along with wrong answers to questions.

And Lord, while you are doing all this for us,
> Help us remember those people
>> Who have few minutes left, not even boring ones,
>>> Who have no opportunity to be public, let alone to blunder,
>> Who have no relationships with others, not even insignificant ones,
>>> Who have no one to listen, let alone to hear them say something stupid.

We pray in the name of the one
> who awoke to bad Fridays and good,
>> Jesus Christ our Lord. Amen.

This Food and These Friends

Ezekiel 34:25-31, Romans 3:21-26

God, we come thanking you
>   for food in a world of hunger,
>   for friendship in a world of loneliness,
>   for education in a world of ignorance,
>   for faith in a world of distrust.

How can it be, God,
>   That we find ourselves so blessed?
Surely not because we are better than others;
>   Our sin is exceeded only by your forgiveness.

Of course we are not complaining, God,
>   Not about this food and these friends.
We have our worries,
>   Some public, most private,
>   That we commend to you this day.

Just now, God, help us
>   Enjoy this food and these friends;
Strengthen even further
>   This community and our faith.

Enable us to use responsibly each of your gifts
>   So that all the families of the earth
>   Might receive blessing,
>   Through Jesus Christ our Lord. Amen.

A Few Pounds Heavier

Exodus 16:1-36, 1 Corinthians 11:17-33

God, we find ourselves holiday rested and a few pounds heavier.
> The rest we needed,
>> The pounds we could do without.
> Of course, God, the food really did taste good,
>> Especially the cookies, the candy, the cake,
>>> the pie, the ice cream.
>> It probably is no mystery, Lord,
>>> where the pounds came from.

Thank you, God, for a sense of taste,
> Help us not to use it tomorrow as we did yesterday.
>> Deliver us from a Big Mac attack,
>>> Or a pasta party.
>> But mostly, God, challenge us not to eat today,
>>> So that tomorrow we may die.

Open our hands and hearts to
> The malnourished who pray each day for at least one meal,
>> The misnourished who can taste only fat, salt and sugar,
> The rigid nutritionists whose taste buds hunt for evil lurking in the food,
>> The ill who want nothing to do with food,
> The recovering whose past diet controls their future meals.

And if you don't mind, next holiday,
> Turn all our digested sugar to vitamin C
>> And our salt to calcium.
> Or if not that,
>> help celery to taste as good as fudge,
>>> And bran flakes like pumpkin pie.

We pray in the name of the one
> who probably lived in a house without digital scales,
>> Jesus Christ our Lord. Amen.

Heard In Our Land

Football

Sports generate interesting traditions, God;
Actions permitted there would not be allowed elsewhere.

You must really enjoy football, God,
Though perhaps for different reasons than we:

Men crashing into each other,
Then getting up and organizing to do it again;
People crowded onto hard benches,
Shivering from the cold,
Cheering at selected crashes;
Others semi-comatose on a couch,
Listening to a voice explain it all,
Interrupted by commercial burps;
Sometimes the men on the field hug each other,
And other activities,
Not encouraged for those watching.

But thank you, God, for football,
Crashing that does not aim to kill,
Touching that does not require explanation,
Sitting that does not need results.

Care for those, Lord,
Who plan only to hurt others,
Who fear touching and being touched,
Who must always be productive.

We pray in the name of the one from Nazareth
who went about touching, calming, and bringing rest,
Jesus Christ our Lord. Amen.

Nightly News

Matthew 6:1-6, Proverbs 12:9

The event is important, God,
  When it appears on the nightly news:

   A family destroyed in an irrational murder/suicide,
      Yen made and dollars lost in the stock market;

   Another "hopeful" running for political office,
      Another cold weather victim of a landlord utility dispute;

   Several dead in a riot seeking to redress oppression,
      Leaders meet to repair the world economy.

Not much good news there, Lord,
  But few people would watch as a reporter announced:
      "Millions were not killed today.
         Almost as many went to work as returned home.
      Most people had food to eat.
         At least half the people smiled sometime during the day."

Thank you, God, for so much that does not make the news,
  Events no one even considers reporting.

   But thank you also for the nightly news,
      A reminder that
         Violence continues to claim victims,
            Many have too little to eat,
         Who gets elected does count,
            Economic systems help some and hurt others.

   Remind us also, God, that your news sounds best
      To those hurt by the events that do make the news,
         Or should make it.
   And your love makes nightly news,
      Less traumatic than might be the case.

We pray in the name of the one
  who came to help the victims of nightly news,
      Jesus Christ our Lord. Amen.

Heard In Our Land

Different Moods

Psalm 139, Matthew 4:1-11

God, it is an unpredictable time of the year.
    Even the weather forecasters end up surprised.
        The temperature is up one day,
            Down the next.
        Yesterday it was up,
            And down today.

Our moods can be like that, Lord.
    We don't show different moods much;
        Sometimes we don't even recognize the changes.
    Thank you, God, for a person or two,
        Who know us well enough to see and respond.
    They give us strength,
        Strength to avoid inflicting our changeableness on
        everyone.

God, people we don't know have cold days too:
    Moments of depression,
        Times of tears;
    Folk we will never meet,
        People we don't even like.

Be with those who have no one to care,
    Or whose culture makes them indifferent.
Be with those who are unaware,
    Or whose whole world seems controlled by emotions.

Lord, provide us all with short sleeves for warm days,
    And a coat for the cold.

We pray in the name of the one
    who also lived an unpredictable life,
        Jesus Christ, our Lord. Amen.

Catalogs

Ecclesiastes 3:1-8, Genesis 1:14-19

The spring seed catalogs just arrived, God,
    Asking me to think garden in the middle of January.
        Next came the summer Sears catalog,
            Requesting that I order short sleeves in zero degree weather.

All that feels beyond me just now,
    The temperature affects my temperament,
        Leaving me a season behind
            The merchandise by Sears and Burpees.

But thank you, God, for an address to give to Penney's,
    Even if I can't buy from them now.
        Be with those who have no winter address,
            And whose clothes come as charity.

Lord, you might send us a warm day or ten,
    So those catalogs won't seem so ridiculous,
But if not, thanks for the winter freeze,
    To prepare the ground for Burpees' beans,
        Which I'll pick when the winter catalog arrives.

We pray in the name of the one for all seasons,
    Jesus Christ our Lord. Amen.

The Journey

Psalm 105:1-45, Hebrews 11:1—12:2

God, we come together anxious for the journey into spring,
Urged on by the early flowers and the greening grass,
And even the less desirable markers of the season,
Like unwanted weeds.
But there is another journey, God,
One stretching as far back as we can see,
flowing as far forward as we can anticipate,
the journey of life.

Sometimes life appears exciting—we sing hymns of praise;
But other times monotonous—we cannot sing at all.

Sometimes we see life ahead—we talk about your emerging kingdom;
But other times mostly death—a tomb with no exit.

Sometimes we can run—and never be weary;
But other times we stumble—and cannot go further.

Sometimes we know the way ahead—and can show others;
But other times we are lost—with no one to help.

God, use our enthusiasm,
Steer our energy,
Enjoy our laughter,
Multiply our numbers
That our journey might enhance life
For those around us,
And those who come after.

God, lift us from the ground,
Light up our darkness,
Wipe away our tears,
Heal our bruises
That our discouragement might not
Destroy the future,
For us and our posterity.

But, God, even now we remember those who describe life
not as a journey,
but only as survival.
Carry them, God,
Carry them on down the road.

We pray in the name of the sojourner from Nazareth,
Jesus Christ our Lord. Amen.

Super Heros

Numbers 13:17-33, Genesis 6:1-4

God, some people certainly are more important than others,
  I feel the difference in my soul.

  I can't spin around in the air
    And slam the ball into a hoop ten feet above the ground.
      Mostly, when I throw my napkin,
        I miss the wastebasket.
  I can't stand in front of a TV camera
    And say anything well enough to get elected president.
      I rarely convince family and friends
        That I know what I'm talking about.
  I can't probe another's body with a beam of light
    And fix things that have gone wrong.
      I only occasionally get a flashlight to work
        When I want it.

  Then of course, God, there are those who have no
    Napkin,
      Family or,
        Flashlight.

It seems, God, that the world is composed of
  Super heros,
    Regular folks,
      Nobodies.
  They really are different,
    One group from the other.

Remind me again, Lord, that there is only one species,
  We all belong to one human-kind.
    We all sleep,
      Though some do it in church instead of at night.
    We all eat,
      Though some have too much and others not enough.
    We all care for other needs
      That are best not mentioned in public prayers.
    We all die,
      Though some make Time magazine and others go
      unnoticed.
Let me not
  Look with awe at another and with shame at myself,
    Glance with disdain at another and with pride at myself.

We pray in the name of the one
  who was just like us and like you,
    Jesus Christ our Lord. Amen.

Days of Our Lives

Joshua 24:1-15, Nehemiah 9:6-38

God, like the sands of an hour glass,
      these are the days of our lives,
    Displayed on daytime soaps,
      And nighttime continuing drama.

It is an interesting world, Lord,
    Slightly different than you intended perhaps,
      Not so different from real life, maybe,
        Except that all the boring moments are missing:

    Their houses always look clean,
      And their cars run.
    They never have to buy groceries,
      Or nurse a sick child.
    They need not take time to study,
      And they never sleep in bed.

Thank you, God, for the boring moments:
    The events that never make the soaps.

    Things we don't have to decide,
      They just have to be done;
    Tasks we don't have to ponder,
      Just shift to neutral and do them;
    Jobs that don't create a crisis,
      We just act.

God, be with those who have no boring moments:
    Each task a crisis,
      Each decision a potential catastrophe.
    It must be exhausting,
      Trying to live out the soaps,
        With no commercials to provide a moment's rest.

And, Lord, be with those who have only boring moments:
    No decisions that go wrong,
      No daring adventures.
    It must be sad,
      When all life's excitement
        Appears on a screen.

Such are the days of our lives,
    And the One who lives in our midst,
      Jesus Christ our Lord. Amen.

Genealogy

Genesis 5:1-32, Matthew 1:1-17

God, families can gather five generations at a reunion,
    The grandchild to the great great grandparent.

    Thanks, for all your children:
        The stories of the eighties,
            The wisdom of the sixties,
        The creativity of the forties,
            The energy of the twenties,
        The hope of the newborn.

    Stay close to all your children:
        The confusion of the eighties,
            The resignation of the sixties,
        The trauma of the forties,
            The frenzy of the twenties,
        The vulnerability of the newborn.

So often, Lord, we find ourselves preoccupied,
    Preoccupied with our own place around the table
        That we ignore the stories of our ancestors
            Until second hand at their wake,
        That we draw away from the diapers of the infant
            Until our waste elimination system breaks down,
        That we grow impatient with the dependency of the old and young
            Until we can't do it ourselves.

Grant us, God, the color of genealogy
    That can live the beauty of those before and behind.
Grant us, God, the fascination of genealogy
    That can learn from those much older and younger.
Grant us, God, the joy of genealogy
    That can laugh and love with all your children.
Grant us, God, the soul of genealogy
    That can feel our heritage and embrace your promise,
        through Jesus Christ our Lord Amen.

Why Go On?

Focus text: *The children struggled together within her; so Rebekah said, "If it be like this, why go on?"*

— Gen. 25:22

Rebekah's cry carries elements of anger and hurt, despair and resignation. Life generates those feelings somedays, many days for some people. The ache may come from physical injury. But at other moments the pain of the world invades the individual's soul. Apparently it was similar for Rebekah. Her pain certainly involved the problems of a difficult pregnancy. However, the text tells us, the ache in Rebekah's womb went beyond the personal. She experienced in the center of her being the trauma of two nations in conflict.

Trauma from our past frequently haunts the present. We search for ways to avoid the pain. If it comes during rest, we try to keep it at bay with activity. If it comes at night, we stay with the day as long as possible. If it shows up at church, some try to cover it with piety. If it breaks through all our defenses, many try to drown it with chemicals.

The interconnected web of the world in which we live exposes us to the horrors of peoples whose place we cannot even locate on a map. We can choose to ignore the suffering of others, but at the cost of numbing our own spirit. When we allow ourselves to touch the world's wounds, we may find within us the fatigue of hunger even if we have food; we may hear the scream of violence even if we have not been struck; we may feel the bondage of drugs even if we are free.

Eventually the time comes when we can no longer avoid the hurt. Tragically some choose a permanent solution to kill the pain and themselves at the same time. But fortunately most realize that even if they cannot rid themselves of a painful past or present, they need not carry the hurt alone. Rebekah brought her anguish into her prayer. So did Job and Jeremiah. So can we. The unhealed hurt, the unforgiven sin, the unrighted wrong belong in our prayer for as long as they fester in our soul.

When one first cries out in prayer, the anguish can feel consuming and uncontrollable, as if there is nothing else to the soul except pain, and so it will always be. However, as we open the wound in prayer, most discover, sometimes slowly, other feelings, emotions that have been blocked by unreleased anguish. We are freed to discover long lost prayers of laughter and love. But those joyful prayers must await another chapter.

Untamed Forces

Job 40:15–41:34, Daniel 7:1-8

God, how does it all fit:
    Elements that have no place,
        Forces that can't be tamed?

    Diseases with a thousand names:
        Latin names,
            Short names,
        No names,
            Deadly names—
    Hidden, silent, indiscriminate.

    Natural disaster from every direction:
        from the clouds,
            from no clouds,
        from the cosmos,
            from deep in the earth—
    intense, sudden, endless.

    Community catastrophe on every side:
        families jammed in a single room,
            people with no one to touch,
    individuals with deadly rage,
        persons driven from needle to bottle.

Does it all belong to you, God:
    The thirsty desert,
        The raging sea,
    The sterile concrete,
        The silent virus?

    Is that the world you love so much,
        You sent your only son,
            Jesus Christ our Lord? Amen.

Not at Our Expense

God, hear our prayer for justice,
    but not at our expense.
That may sound flippant, Lord,
    perhaps even sinful when we say it.

We admit that we are the powerful on the earth;
    We gained that position by birth
        rather than talent
            or goodness.

It may even be that the world situation would improve
    if others were in charge instead of us,
        at least some of us.

But it is hard to pray for justice, God,
    if that prays us into oblivion
        or at least poverty.
    It feels like that's what you want sometimes:
        "Sell all you have."

Let it be if that must happen,
    but until then, God,
        Show us how to use our power
            to step aside to let others lead,
                to soften the blow when trouble strikes,
            to stand up when groups are misused,
                to quiet the storm when anger destroys,
            to lift the load when another stumbles,
                to bind up when nature is wounded.

In the name of the one from Galilee,
    who was both king and peasant,
        Jesus Christ our Lord. Amen.

I'm not Sure What She Expects

Matthew 7:7-12, James 5:13-15

She asked me to remember her, God,
    Remember her in prayer.

    But I'm not sure what she expects from that, Lord,
        Maybe a miracle, maybe just not to be forgotten.

    The latter I can offer
        And ask of you, God:

        In the midst of all that I have to do,
            Help me to remember those who count on my care.

        I cannot even imagine all those that need your touch.
            Remember them, Lord,
                If that is not overwhelming for you,
                    As it appears to me.

But, God, I think she wanted an end to her trouble,
    And hoped that my prayer would accomplish that.

        I'm not sure what to do with that hope,
            Perhaps you are not either.

        Maybe we can help her find a way through,
            Though you may need a different servant than me.
        I can't really see the way.

        Open a door in the walls of her life,
            Or help her live as best she can in the space she
            has.

    And God, help me know better what to say
        When I'm asked to remember a friend in prayer.

We pray in the name of the one who taught us to pray,
    Jesus Christ our Lord. Amen.

You Must Get Weary

God, the world is still anxious and angry,
    Throwing words at each other and sometimes more.

    Bystanders function as bait
        To bully an adversary.
    Children lie in their own blood
        To pay back an enemy.

It is like on the playground and in the hallway,
    Behavior we assume children outgrow.

You must get weary, Lord.
    We do.
        And afraid.
The world is not an elementary school,
    The weapons are not fists.

God, in the middle of a world that fans the fires of hate,
    A people that seem to know no other way,

    Take us deep inside
        Where we want revenge
            For injustice and abuse.
    Teach us how to act on those feelings,
        So as not to bury hate and ignore anger,
            But neither ignite in others the feelings that seethe
            in us.

Oh, God who hears the cries of the oppressed,
    who feels the pain of the abused,
        who knows the darkness of those destroyed,
    Don't give up on us yet.
        Help us find a way
            That the hater and the hated can eat together,
            And the world of someday can be today.

We pray in the name of the one whose body and blood transforms hatred
    into communion, Jesus Christ our Lord. Amen.

Justice Is so Ordinary

Jeremiah 7:1-7, Proverbs 21:3,15

God, justice is so ordinary,
    so unexciting and everyday.

        Of course it is important when we are the victim,
            when we are the ones crying, "Unfair,"

        Like when a sister gets more candy than we get,
            Or a brother drank all the pop.

        Like when another person takes credit for work we did,
            Or we get trashed by unspoken expectations.

But mostly, God, justice does not stir our passion;
    It deals with people far away or events of short duration.

        Is there something we are missing in that
            More central than candy or even land distribution:

        Justice that we can understand down deep,
            That rises out of the very soul of a people;

        Justice that we can taste in the tear of a child,
            Or see in the lined face of a farmer;

        Justice that we can hear in the agony of our own hurt,
            Or find in the ruins of a relationship?

Grant us a passion for justice,
    Not as a selfish demand or strident cause,
        But as a way to live quietly with everyone,
            In the manner of the one from Nazareth,
                Jesus Christ our Lord. Amen.

Some More Enlisted

Judges 5:1-31, 2 Kings 25:1-7

God, some more enlisted today,
    Expecting to be veterans in the future.

    They enlisted for a lot of reasons:
        a good job,
            a desire for adventure,
                family tradition,
            a sense of responsibility,
        boredom with their lives.

    Now there are others for the President to deploy,
        The General Secretary can send them to wherever

        to keep the peace,
            to defend our honor,
                to protect freedom,
                to bring justice,
            to prove we can't be pushed around,
        to die.

Why, God, do you give people the power to decide life and death
    from an office in Moscow or Washington or Pretoria or Jerusalem.

    The young people didn't enlist
        thinking they would die,
            not really knowing why.
    They thought that there would be no fighting,
        or they would be spared,
            or you would protect them.

Lord, we place in your hands those who have died;
    Please care for them better than we did.

    And help us to use our power
        To settle disputes without burying people,
            To stop evil without firing rockets,
        To effect justice without caskets,
            To demonstrate strength without destruction.

We pray in the name of the one who gave his life
    so that we would not have to take others,
        Jesus Christ our Lord. Amen.

It Is Not All Our Fault

Exodus 1:8-22, Isaiah 1:21-23

God, the world is a pretty mixed up place;
    many people have little chance to enjoy it.

        Hunger preoccupies the child,
            drugs dictate the day for many.

        A knock in the night terrifies the family,
            the flash from a handgun brings instant darkness.

        Death rattles from the sky,
            the road explodes into a grave.

We can't escape responsibility, Lord;
    Some is our fault:

        the taxes we don't want to pay, but do,
            the stock purchased by our insurance;

        the cheap tennies from K-Mart,
            the cola spit out by the machine;

        the banana we peel,
            the coffee we taste.

But God, it is not all our fault:

    Don't let us be paralyzed by guilt
        That comes despite our deepest yearning,
            That eludes our most courageous action.

    Help us find our way to a world
        without murder,
            or empty stomach,
        a time when all have tennies,
            or maybe even better.

We pray in the name of the one who found a way
    through the Roman world and a cross,
        Jesus Christ our Lord. Amen.

The One Beside Me

Jonah 1:1-16, Matthew 16:13-23

God, who is the person next to me,
    The one across the room?
        Why do they act as they do?

They are not among the real crazies in the world,
    The ones that cause us to recoil in horror:

        Who shoot up synagogues,
            Who rape women,
                Who violate children;
        Who sell addictive drugs,
            Who crush the poor,
                Who torture the peasant.

    It feels hopeless
        to see life through the eyes
            Of the psychotic.

Do you understand them, God?

But, Lord, what about the normal people,
    Maybe like us,
        The one beside me:

        Why all those tears?
            Could she tell me if I asked?
        Why so silent and anxious?
            What does he fear from this group?
        Why call attention to herself?
            Is she often left out?

God, grant that we might never stop wondering about each other,
    But help us discern the difference between wonder and meddling.
        Teach us when to leave the other person to you,
            And turn our attention to those we can help.

We pray in the name of the one from Nazareth,
    Who cares for the crazy and those less so,
        Jesus Christ our Lord. Amen.

Your World Has Been Ruined

Genesis 6:11-13 ; 8:1-5, Hosea 11:1-9

God, who can stand before your anger?
> Who can survive your wrath?
>> The reasons for divine rage are clear enough.

Your world has been ruined:
> The rain intended to bathe the earth
>> Eats the trees,
> Relationships designed to foster companionship
>> Promote loneliness,
> Ground designed to teem with life
>> Lies buried beneath asphalt,
> Sexuality intended for creation and play
>> Explodes in shame and exploitation.

God, we come with no excuse for this destruction,
> Though it is not hard to blame others,
>> Those who have gone before us,
>>> Leaving a world on the edge of chaos,
>> Those who, unlike us,
>>> Refuse to acknowledge the world as your gift.

> Except we can't explain all the mess
>> As the actions of the deceased and the pagans.

> Remember not, God, the sin of others and of us.
>> Remember instead the pain of your people,
>>> The wounded and the injured,
>>>> Those adrift and passionless.
>>> Remember, God,
>>>> Remember the pain of the world,
>>> The human and the non-human.

We pray in the name of the one through whose spirit your memory works,
> Jesus Christ our Lord. Amen.

Why Go On?

The City Suffers

The city suffers this day, God,
    Drowning in a sea of pain.

    Some is self-inflicted:
        Circles of vengeance
            Motivated by honor or glory;
        Artificial happiness
            Purchased on the street corner.

    Much is inflicted by outsiders:
        Fear of city folk whose language differs,
            Or whose skin needs no tan;
        Visitors that delight in city services,
            But return home to avoid the problems.

God, all the suffering that has ever been,
    Can be found in the city this day.

    We look from a distance,
        Willing to venture only a little,
    Concerned that we too might be swallowed up
        By problems that defy solutions.

    Urban violence feeds the morgue,
        How long, O Lord?
    Hopelessness lies in the doorway,
        Will it last forever, God?

    Is the city more than you can handle?
        Do tears of anguish still reach your ears?

We pray in the name of the one who died
    just outside the city,
        Jesus Christ our Lord. Amen.

Violence or Art

I Samuel 4:1-22, Genesis 35:16-20

God,
    The surfer falls artistically
        from the balcony,
    The model collapses poetically
        with a hole in her swimsuit,
    The people bounce around musically
        as the bomb explodes,
    The sky erupts with a new cloud
        where an object had flown.

Lord, it is sometimes hard to tell violence from art:

    Death that recovers with a Big Mac or Diet Pepsi,
        From death that creates widows and orphans,
    Death that will happen again next week on TV,
        From death that creates lonely weeks without end.

It seems confusing:

    Should we eat popcorn,
        or say a prayer;
    Should we record the music,
        or turn to a hymn;
    Should we be sickened,
        or sexually teased;
    Should we weep,
        or turn to the same station next week.

It is probably beyond straightening out, God;
    So please,
        Sit beside those watching television.
            Take the hand of those crying at the wake,
                through Jesus Christ our Lord. Amen.

No Cards

Job 3:1-26, Psalm 88:1-18

God, no cards stand in the rack
>To celebrate the day of ones own death,
>>Cards with funny phrases,
>>>Or beautiful pictures.

Many wish for such a card
>To send to themselves.
They long for death,
>Not suicide with attendant anger and guilt,
>>Nor murder with its violation and violence,
But death given as mysteriously as life,
>Perhaps egg and sperm simply going separate ways,
>>As hidden from view as first they came together.

Ought one pray for death?
>Perhaps not.
>>Many do.

God, be with those today
>For whom death seems more to be treasured than life;
>>For whom childhood evokes only nightmares;
>For whom the future anticipates only pain;
>>For whom the coffin feels like the softest bed;

Provide life, Lord,
>Satisfying enough that all can celebrate
>>the day of their birth,
>Restful enough that all can delight in
>>the night of their conception.

But if that can't be, God,
>Grant those the rest they need,
>>Through Jesus Christ our Lord. Amen.

Heard In Our Land

The Winter Is Past

Focus text:

For lo, the winter is past,
The rains are over and gone.
Flowers appear on the earth,
The time of singing comes.
The coo of the dove
Is heard in our land.

— Song of Songs 2:11-12

Life brings moments of deep joy. Love is at the center of many such moments, the love which the woman and man sing to one another in the Song of Songs. I call it joy, but I mean much more than joy. I refer to that sense of inner shalom that enables one to sing with H.G. Spafford, "It is well, it is well with my soul."

Sometimes this joy literally explodes from within. I can tell another about that joy. I can even express it physically through a hug or a shout. Yet somehow our joy can never adequately be expressed. This happens of course when the joy I feel is missing in those around me. It also occurs because the explosion of joy deep within me, exceeds my means for expression.

Of course not all joy wants to explode outward. Sometimes this shalom flows inward, carrying me ever deeper into my center. There it remains quietly, visible only to a few, expressed best in silence or perhaps a gentle touch, maybe a deep breath.

The words of prayer similarly dilute the emotion of joy. Yet the experience that the "winter is past" wants to be communicated to God as well as to one another.

Deep Within Us

Mark 12:28-34, Song of Songs 7:10-13

God, love stirs deep within us:
    The comfort we find in family,
        The bond we live with our child,
    The desire we experience for another,
        The affection we feel for a friend.

Thank you, God, for the love that surges through our body.

    Of course sometimes it surges the wrong way;
        We hold when we ought to release,
            Run away when we should run toward.

    Forgive us for embracing love in ways that damage others.
        Enable us to pardon one another for such hurt,
            Rather than act out our pain
                To punish or destroy.

God, your love moves powerfully between us:
    The food and medicine that flow to drought and disaster,
        The hospitality that receives a stranger,
    The retaliation that does not happen,
        The hand that lifts the fallen.

Thank you, God for your love that mists between us.

    Of course sometimes we blow it away,
        Channeling it only to those we like,
            Or inhaling it all ourselves.

    Forgive us for misdirecting your love.
        Free us from the desire to control it,
            The love that originates in you,
                destined for people we can't or won't touch.

Thank you, for love, God,
    within and between us.
        May we never leave home without it.

We pray in the name of the one
    through whom we know your love,
        Jesus Christ our Lord. Amen.

A Moment's Rest

Genesis 26:12-33, Matthew 11:28-30

God, thank you for a moment's rest amid the tension of every day.
    Many people can never rest:

        Those who spend each moment searching for something to eat,
            And those fighting to stay on their diet;
        Those whose eyes constantly search for a warm place to sleep,
            And those who resent cleaning their house;
        Those who fear every moment having their illiteracy discovered,
            And those who dread keeping up with their studies;

        Those whose heart aches for lost loved ones,
            And those weary of constant fighting with their family;
        Those who long for someone with whom to share life,
            And those who wish their spouse were dead;
        Those who wait each month to see if they are pregnant,
            And those forced to care for yet another child.

Sometimes, God, we are those unrested people.
    That makes all the more precious the moments of rest
        you build in the world around us:

        Snow drifting down with the wind,
            Nighttime traffic following its allotted course;
        Embrace of a friend following a quarrel,
            A soft pillow at the end of the day;

        An evening alone without feeling lonely,
            Time with a loved one at home;
        The warmth of friendly silence,
            Carried by music to a new place.

God, provide for those who never know them,
        moments of rest.
    Grant to those too busy,
        the breath of life.
    Give to those too anxious,
        rest from their labor.

We pray in the name of the one
    who came that we might have rest for the soul,
        Jesus Christ our Lord. Amen.

Happily Ever After

Genesis 33:1-17,   Luke 15:11-32

God, thank you for stories that end happily ever after,
Well at least that conclude with people back together again:

For families who find each other
After years of estrangement.

For individuals who laugh again
After oceans of tears.

For neighbors who loan each other lawn tools
After complaining about dogs, kids, and trash.

For friends who hug each other
After weeks of being careful about feelings.

For nations who retool their munitions plants to farm equipment
After generations of hostilities.

Lord, we know not every story has a happy ending,
Some must learn to live always in pain,

The anguish of unending alienation,
The weariness of constant fighting;

The fear of complete destruction,
The anxiety of utter failure.

Be with them, God.
Care for their stories, too.

Give them peace at some moments,
Satisfaction in others.

Give us all stories to tell
That let us walk together.

We pray in the name of the one from Nazareth,
Whose story was pretty grim,
But whose ending generates hope for all stories,
Jesus Christ, our Lord. Amen.

Secret Power

Genesis 24:1-67, Luke 24:13-35

God, power often operates in secret places.
    Influence hides from sight.

    We are used to hidden power in public politics,
        Smoke filled rooms, payoffs, favoritism,
            Speeches that hide more than reveal.

    We have been victims of secret power between persons,
        Deception that leaves us confused,
            Hidden decisions that render us helpless.

Lord, not all silent influence is oppressive.
    Sometimes hidden strength is welcome:

    The abiding power of the quiet presence
        To balance the competing claims of the noisy.

    The determined planning of the quiet figure
        To make the dreams of others work.

    The calming words of the quiet member
        To ease the tension of the angry.

Thank you, God, for strength from unexpected people
    To sustain us when our visible energy runs out.
Thank you, Lord, for direction from unnoticed persons
    To guide us when we feel lost in life.

Forgive us all,
    The loud and the quiet,
        The private and the public,
    When we use our power to make our own life better,
        At the expense of those less strong.

We pray in the name of the one from Nazareth,
    Whose power few understand,
        But through whose strength all are made alive,
            Jesus Christ our Lord. Amen.

Metaphor

Isaiah 40:1-11, Ezekiel 37:1-14

Thank you, God, for metaphor,
    For picture language,

    Carrying us to new places
        With familiar words,

        Worlds we can never visit,
           Worlds past or future,
        Worlds even so where people
        Live and love,
           Work and die,

    For metaphor that transports us to new feelings,

        Emotions we might never touch,
           Emotions buried deep inside,
        Emotions even so that help us understand
        Ourselves, and
        Those unlike us.

Thank you God, for poetry and song,
    For story and painting,
        Opening the creation that nurtures us
        And the evil that frightens us.

    Help us teach others
        to sing,
           to write poetry,
             to tell stories:

One whose soul has been drowned
    in a multitude of tasks;
Whose vision has been narrowed
    by the opinions that run our world;
Whose compassion has been limited
    by an assigned role.

We pray in the name of the one from Nazareth,
    whose stories opened new vistas to the hurt,
        whose poetry created new possibilities for the numb,
        Jesus Christ our Lord. Amen.

Precious Learnings

Proverbs 10:1-9, Deuteronomy 6:20-25

Thank you, God,
  For those who share their experience,
    the most precious learnings from their life:

  How to trim trees
    And enjoy a meal;

  How to plant seeds
    And play with a lover;

  How to care for a friend
    And respond to hate;

  How to express anger
    And mend torn clothing.

Grant us, God, patience,

  Patience to persist with he who has little wisdom,
    To continue with she who ignores experience.

  She stomps on sensibilities,
    He tramples beauty.
  He doesn't know dirty from clean,
    Nor she courtesy from gross.

Grant us, Lord, courage,

  Courage to share our deepest knowing,
    To offer our most precious wisdom,
  Though it be rejected by some,
    And ignored by others.

We pray in the name of the one
  who grew in wisdom, stature, and favor,
    Jesus Christ our Lord. Amen.

The Sense of Taste

God, thank you for food,
    Indispensable to our life,
        Though probably not in the quantities we inhale.

Thank you for the sense of taste,
    Activated at the mere thought of food,
        Though seldom for the most nutritious cuisine.

Thank you that we don't all like the same food.
    Somebody has to like liver,
        Or we would have to breed cows without livers.

Thank you for holidays that feature food,
    A few more would be nice,
        As long as they celebrated foods I like.

Lord, stay close to those who swallow their food without tasting,
    Not just because they may need the Heimlich maneuver;
        Something must be terribly wrong
            to pass up one of life's greatest pleasures.
Of course if they are guests in someone's home
    And are served something they don't like,
        Then help them swallow without tasting.

Care for those who prepare food,
    Especially food that is best not tasted.
        They probably don't like their job
            Any more than we like their food.

Chide those who care only for taste, ignoring nutrition.
    They cut down the length of time we can enjoy food,
        Trading heart trouble later for sugar and salt now.

Help those preoccupied with nutrition.
    They may die of heart failure with a frown on their face,
        Reading the nutritional content of my favorite food.

We pray in the name of the one from Galilee
    who ate almost everyday of his life,
        never once at a fast food place,
            Jesus Christ our Lord. Amen.

Made Out of Dirt

Genesis 2:4-15, Isaiah 41:17-20

God, some days the earth is warm and moist,
    Gardens exist so that adults can play in warm dirt.

    Other days the earth is soggy and heavy,
        Sticks to the shoes, the shovel and the dog.

    Then there are the days the earth is hot and parched,
        Can't much more than dent it with a swing of the pick.

God, people resemble the dirt a lot,
    Not in how they look or act exactly,
        But in how they feel from day to day.

Thank you, God, for the warm and moist people:
    The ones who invite us in
        To love and to laugh,
            To care and to cry.
    Grant us many days
        when we feel warm and moist inside.

Help us, God, deal with the cold and soggy people,
    The ones who invite us in,
        And then we are stuck.
            No way to leave except with great effort.
    Blow a warm drying breeze through us
        those days when we feel like cold, soggy mud.

Help us, God, reach the hot and parched people,
    The ones who invite no one in,
        But hide inside a sun-dried wall
            Lest they be hurt or soiled.
    Rain gently on us
        those days when we feel like hot, parched dust.

We pray in the name of the one
    formed out of dirt just like us,
        Jesus Christ our Lord. Amen.

Cold Weather

Genesis 1:1-3, 26-31, Psalm 150

God, it seems appropriate today to be thankful for warm things;
    Much colder and our thanks may freeze unspoken.

Thank you, God, for:

    Human creativity
        that enables us to adapt to various climates,
            temperatures we are not genetically equipped to
            survive;

    Warm beings,
        people who warm our souls as well as our bodies,
            teddy bears, dogs and cats to cuddle when people
            turn cold;

    Divine touch
        providing a bright moon on a frigid night,
            making the snow appear like a covering of warm
            marshmallow;

    Compassionate people
        opening churches, schools, shopping centers,
            to those unable to provide their own heat.

    Super cold days
        that provide occasion to wear coats, sweaters,
            hats, gloves, scarves, long underwear all at once.

We are thankful for all these things, God,
    And probably some others that we are too cold to remember.

We pray in the name of the one from Nazareth
    who managed in cold weather too,
        hopefully not so cold that he needed a ski mask,
            Jesus Christ our Lord. Amen.

Those Who Have Gone Before

Matthew 1:1-16,   Genesis 25:8-10,   Genesis 35:27-29

Thank you, God, for those who have gone before us,
  Whose saga we can retell.

  Some were favored by circumstances,
    And occasionally by you.

  Others seemed always blocked by their own behavior,
    Or the actions of another.

  We rejoice at their moments of triumph and faithfulness,
    We hurt at the misuse of power and the lack of trust.

God, we too will leave a saga for those who follow,
  Even if our name is lost after this generation or the next.

    Our choice would be that we be a part of your story of
    blessing.
      But if not, remember us as you remembered Ishmael,
      Esau, and Leah.

    We commend our saga into your safe keeping.
      Extend to us the same patience you showed to Jacob
      and Laban.

We pray in the name of the one from Nazareth
  who cared for the sinners as well as the saints,
    and for those who were a mixture of the two,
      Jesus Christ our Lord. Amen

Eyes Open

Focus text:

> *The wise have their eyes open,*
> *The fool walks in darkness.*
> *Yet, I perceive,*
> *A common fate awaits them both.*

— Qoheleth, Ecclesiastes 2:14

For the most part we ignore the "preacher" (*Qoheleth* in Hebrew) in Ecclesiastes. Qoheleth has trouble seeing a clear path through life. The rules learned from tradition do not seem to hold as he (presumably a "he") observes the world around him. He tries to discern the "rules" that govern the natural and moral world, but cannot find the answer to life's most difficult questions (1:12-14). Justice gets trampled in the market place (1:22). The oppressed find no deliverer, often no one to comfort them (4:1). People pile up wealth without ever being satisfied (4:8).

Perhaps we will not reach the level of despair we feel in Qoheleth. Surely, however, as we raise our deepest questions in prayer, we cannot fail to wonder about many of the same things that troubled Qoheleth. I find the world perplexing. Occasionally I see what I believe is justice prevail. But sometimes what appears to be justice in one moment later proves to be injustice or gets perverted in some way. Once in a while I catch a glimpse of what I understand to be harmony within the human community and with nature. So often that evaporates and what seemed like harmony one moment looks distorted the next.

I suppose we could transfer justice and harmony from this world to the "next," or from the present to the distant future. But that takes God out of our life, limiting God's active presence to another realm or time. That is not the way I read the biblical faith. Hence sometimes the deepest prayer expresses life's confusion, a complexity that seems to defy solution, even laughs at the "obvious" solutions people suggest.

Electromania

Ezekiel 36:22-28, Exodus 23:12

It is crazy, God,
    Electromania.

    What doesn't show up on a computer screen
        Doesn't exist.
            People can be lost in a thirty second power
            outage,
                Their names blotted from the face of the earth
                    when the monitor goes black.
            They may as well pack it in;
                the data can't be recovered.

    What can't be cooked in a microwave
        Is not edible.
            Whole recipe books become instant antiques;
                no one can boil water anymore.
            The only safe food
                glows in the dark.

    Reality happens only on the video screen,
        Where it can be replayed upside down and backwards.
            If the cassette jams,
                the car chase may never end.
            If the satellite goes berserk,
                we'll likely miss the Second Coming.

But, God,
    We notice a few loose ends,
        A little left untended so far:
    Computerized soul doesn't satisfy,
        Microwaved care tends to wilt,
            The spirit can't be transmitted well by satellite.

Lord,
    Until we can solve these slight problems,
        Commend to electronics these minor irritations.
    Grant us the relic of a non-computerized soul;
        Help us remember how to care by human touch;
            Send out your spirit the old fashioned way.

By the way, God, if this prayer is lost, stolen or forgotten,
    I'll sent you the computer disk
        Indexed under the name of Jesus Christ our Lord. Amen.

Our Leaders

Jonah 1:1-16, Judges 9:7-15

God, it appears that leaders cause most of our turmoil.
It is hard not to be cynical when we look around.
Perhaps if we hurl them overboard it would calm things
down.

God, it appears we have only two choices.
Which is better: incompetent or obstinate.

Leaders who use their power to destroy,
Or those who seem to self destruct?

Leaders who smash down doors that stand in their way,
Or those who forget to open a door before walking through?

Those who plot institutional hegemony,
Or those who cannot pronounce the word?

Except, God, even in our anger and laughter,
complaints and derision about our leaders,
We notice a problem:
Our leaders act a lot like us,

Perhaps had you better give us a dish full of compassion,
Instead of the Hoover to sweep away all leaders.
Teach us to feed the leaders we criticize
In order that we too might be satisfied.

We pray in the name of the leader from Galilee,
Jesus Christ our Lord. Amen.

Coveting

Exodus 20:17, 2 Samuel 12:1-6

Lord, we read: "You shall not covet,"
  Or in an older translation: "Thou shalt not covet."

  We have been told that means
    I should not want my neighbor's new car
      Instead of my old one.
  But I do want my neighbor's car.
    You would to, God,
      If you looked at the cars side by side.

  Be that as it may, Lord,
    Forgive me for wanting my neighbors' car
      And their other car as well.

Actually, God, my neighbor's car is pretty safe,
  Mine still runs even without a sunroof.

But, Lord, the society in which we live
  Appears more confusing.
    Fueled by desire,
      It runs on acquisition.
  Coveting generates jobs;
    Not coveting causes recessions.
      This commandment appears anti-American.

Help us find another way, God,
  Beyond desire,
    Instead of coveting.
  But in the meantime,
    We need a lot of forgiveness.
  My neighbor just saw an advertisement
    For a home entertainment center,
      And my speakers deliver mostly static.

We pray in the name of the One from Nazareth,
  Who had no desire for a car,
    But did want a donkey and a colt for the parade,
      Jesus Christ our Lord. Amen.

Privacy

Genesis 3:8-13, Psalm 139

Our life can be so private, God.
    We can hide so very much
        from our brothers and sisters.

    Thank you for that privacy, Lord.
        It keeps us from being publically accountable
            for all we think and feel.
        It gives us a chance to start over
            in new places and times.
        It enables us to fantasize outrageous things
            and go on living responsibly.

    Help us not to misuse that cloak of privacy, God,
        To mislead others
            about our real intentions,
        To stay in our own world,
            avoiding the problems around us,
        To stave off intimacy,
            leaving others standing alone.

Yet our life can be too public, God.
    We stand exposed to
        judgment, ridicule, laughter.

    Protect us from too much publicity:
        every move watched,
            every action analyzed,
        every event subject to others' conversation,
            every mistake journalistic copy.

    Help us to give ourselves to others openly,
        Not holding back out of fear,
            Willing to risk being misunderstood,
        Asking for what we need,
            Trusting that love is there for us.

We pray in the name of the one
    who revealed your private world for all the world
        to see, to use, even to abuse,
            Jesus Christ our Lord. Amen.

For Freedom

Genesis 2:16-17,   Galatians 5:13-14

Thank you, God, for freedom,
　　for permission to work and play in your world,

　　To plant, cultivate, even trample,
　　　　To write, preach, even joke,
　　　　　　To play, laugh, even lie,
　　　　　　　　To compete, cooperate, even cheat,

　　　　　　　　To throw a ball, a frisbee, even food,
　　　　　　To run, wrestle, even loaf,
　　　　To daydream, pray, even fantasize,
　　To touch, feel, even punch.

Thank you, God, for freedom,
　　for permission to do what we want in your world.

Except, Lord, what about all the limitations.
　　Mostly we see prohibition:

　　Don't drive too fast,
　　　　or dress too showy.
　　Don't spend too much,
　　　　or love the wrong person.

　　Don't write incorrectly,
　　　　or pray irreverently.
　　Don't use the wrong word,
　　　　or work for the wrong company.

We see all these restrictions, God,
　　things we should do or ought not.

We need your help, God,
　　to find a way through the
　　　　go signs,
　　　　　　stop signals,
　　　　　　　　caution lights,
　　to make freedom real,
　　　　and responsibility genuine.

We pray in the name of the one
　　who in your freedom became flesh and lived among us,
　　　　Jesus Christ our Lord. Amen.

The Family Knows

Lord, odd things happen in families;
    Sometimes abusive would be more accurate.

Family members talk a good line,
    but that is for public consumption;
        the real meaning lies hidden from view.
The family knows what really happens,
    but they won't tell,
        not even one another.

It is a game we play, God,
    To maintain the appearance of propriety,
        While acting out our deepest needs
            or our darkest impulses.

Occasionally it is right, Lord,
    To keep the family functioning,
        So that it does not break under the weight
            of normal conflict or cruel honesty.

But then you know all that, God.
    You see the public face and the private intention.
You understand the shadow of our private worlds,
    But you seldom tell on us either.

Forgive us, when we lose our way,
    And make victims out of family members
        By our private maneuvers.
Grab our attention, stop us
    When actions change from scheming
        To violation and violence.

Be with those who can't negotiate a path
    Through such a maze
        And reject the family, angrily.
And be with those, God, who have no family
    To work along side in public,
        And work around in private.

We pray in the name of the one from Galilee,
    who knows the hidden secrets of the heart,
        Jesus Christ our Lord. Amen

Are We Necessary?

Jonah 4:1-11, Job 7:6-10

God, are we really necessary?
    Do we help write the script all the way to the end?

    Or does the future really rest in your hands,
        We being more convenient than crucial?

    Our confessions of faith point in your direction;
        Your will be done on earth as it is in heaven.

God, we don't want to run the whole show.
    We know what goes on when we are completely in charge.

    We put twelve socks in the washer and retrieve eleven.
        We pour coffee over cereal.
            Eggs explode with one little crack.

    If we were in charge of the universe,
        We might forget to turn the seasons,
            Or change the sprinkler.
        We might misplace a star,
            Or spill a galaxy.

No, God, it's best that we not be in charge,
    But we want to be important,
        Not irreplaceable
            But not interchangeable either.

We pray in the name
    of the incomparable one from Nazareth,
        Jesus Christ our Lord. Amen.

Ill Fitted

Genesis 29:31–30:24, 1 Samuel 1:1-20

God, the tears of the unwed mother won't stop.
>They mix with the tears of one who can't have children.

How does it happen, Lord.
>So many people,
>>Their life incomplete
>>>Or ill fitted for this time and place:

The blind woman trying to live in a world
>of television, video games and catalogs,

The deaf man listening to the silence of a world
>run by telephone and soothed by music,

The heavy child carrying the weight of a world
>filled with mirrors, cruel jokes and beautiful bodies,

The mentally slow youth hunting for work in a world
>of computers, robots and laboratories.

So many, God, who just don't fit in our world,
>Trying to cope,
>>Longing for the missing piece.

We hurt with them.
>Sometimes we are them.
>>We usually hide our ill fitting pieces,
>>>Our lack less obvious than theirs.

Forgive us, Lord;
>Still we help dream of a world
>>that suits mostly us.
Comfort us, God;
>We too hurt
>>in a standardized world.
Help us, Lord,
>Be willing to give up a world
>>so poorly matched to others and to us.

We pray in the name of the Galilean
>who included people others left out,
>>Jesus Christ our Lord. Amen.

Change

Isaiah 43:18-19, Ecclesiastes 3:2-8

God, one day is not like the last,
　　However endlessly they drone on.
　　　　One day we meet a beginning,
　　　　　　The next find ourselves at an end.

God, we confess your presence in each beginning,
　　And bestow your blessing on each departure.

　　Except that misses our reality.
　　　　It sounds easier than it feels.

　　Many beginnings feel ominous,
　　　　Initiated by chance, demand, even force.
　　The departures often leave us abandoned.
　　　　Things we love evaporate with no tomorrow.

God, change can wound our soul.
　　The heart doesn't flip as easily as the calendar;
　　　　Even you can slip from sight in transition.

Forgive us when our motor refuses to start
　　When you call.
　　　　Jump start us
　　　　　　If you must.

Calm us when our hopes for "always"
　　Crash into their end.
　　　　Help us begin again
　　　　　　When we must.

And God, comfort us when our present
　　vanishes into your past.
　　　　Carry us
　　　　　　in your arms.

We pray in the name of the one
　　in whom all ends become beginnings—eventually at least,
　　　　Jesus Christ our Lord. Amen.

In the Same World

Genesis 1:27,   Genesis 2:21-25

What are we to do, God,
    Women and men in the same world?

    Switch places for a while?
        Put women in charge?
            Let men be violated?
            Many deserve it.

    Reduce life to thoughts and skills?
        Not notice beauty
            Except in the right time, place, and person?

What are we to do, God,
    Rich and poor in the same world?

    Give most money to the poor?
        Let the formerly rich
            Be angry, hopeless, called lazy?
            Many deserve it.

    Give everyone just enough
        So we will all be the same,
            Clones of the same zygote?

It is not, God, like we have been wise,
    Doing the best we know
        To live together.

    Our actions have proved foolish
        more often than wise.
            Our behavior often alienating
            rather than reconciling.

Still, God, treat us gently
    As we struggle with
        the traditions which formed us.

    Lead us on new paths:
        Women and men,
            Rich and poor,
                In the same world
                    together.

We pray in the name of the one
    who walked boldly down new roads,
        Jesus Christ our Lord. Amen

Poetry and Science

Genesis 1:1-31, Job 38:1–41:34

God, poetry and science,
    How do those two go together?
        They seem like such different worlds.

    The poet doesn't work very well constrained by data, Lord.
        The eye can seldom verify what the poet understands.
    The scientist needs the predictable world,
        A world that everyone finds the same.

Of course we need them both, God.
    It would be hard to drive to the store in a poetic metaphor,
        Embarrassing to go to church dressed in a simile.
    It is silly to describe a rose with a chemical equation,
        Impossible to reduce love to a mathematical formula.

But with truth, God, matters become more confusing.
    Which one can provide us real truth:
        The short story
            Or the test tube?

Help us to look for you, God,
    In the experiment of the scientist,
        In the art of the poet.

Help us to receive your word, Lord,
    Whether through the eye of a microscope
        Or the drama of a song.

And lead us not into temptation,
    Rejecting the scientist as unconcerned,
        Ignoring the poet as unthinking,
    Discarding the relevance of the poem,
        Dismissing the care of technology.

We pray in the name of the carpenter/poet from Nazareth,
    Jesus Christ our Lord. Amen.

Unmade

Jeremiah 20:7-12, John 20:1-29

God:
> There are moments when we feel unmade,
>> Trashed like a bed after a pillow fight.

> There are times we feel unheld,
>> With the self-image of a dropped egg.

> There are moments we feel out of power,
>> All the drive of a dead battery.

> There are times we feel lost,
>> Stamped with a non-existent zip code.

Lord, it's a wonder that you can find us
> In all our crevices, canyons and catastrophes:

> But thank you for
>> attending to unmade beds,
>>> picking up dropped eggs,
>> recharging exhausted batteries,
>>> accepting unclaimed mail.

> And if possible, God,
>> Keep us from being a disaster
>>> Waiting to happen.

We pray in the name of the one
> who picks up the fallen
>> and reclaims the lost,
>>> Jesus Christ our Lord. Amen.

The Beginning of Knowledge

Focus text:

The fear of the Lord is the beginning of knowledge;
Fools despise wisdom and learning.

— The sage, Proverbs 1:7

The sage in ancient Israel experienced the presence of God in all life, from the regular rotation of the seasons to the movement of history. Hence wisdom finds its center in the acknowledgment of the presence of God. That acknowledgment does not inhibit growth and learning, according to the sage, but in fact necessitates continuing investigation and discernment in God's world.

Growth, new ideas, change frequently frighten us. Rather than following the discernment of Israel's ancient sages, we often prefer a more static understanding of life. In that case we decide to learn only what others have already discovered. After all, we conclude, life remains the same yesterday, today and tomorrow.

This static view, probably unfairly attributed to early Greek philosophy, can cause us to misuse the literature of Israel's sages. We often interpret the sages' proverbs as ossified chunks of truth rather than observations of life based on experience. On the one hand this petrified view of the proverbs causes us to over-value the proverbs, using them as rocks to be slung at any one who suggests something new. On the other hand, by not acknowledging divine presence that provides new wisdom as well as old understandings, we have been foolish, according to the sage.

Of course we are very willing to admit that God is at the center of growth and change when the growth happens to someone else. If the change happens to me, I do not mind if it comes in a part of my life that does not seriously threaten my truth. In addition I have no trouble acknowledging to God, as I pray, that I have much to learn. However I become irritated when I must confront the really new that forces me to give up my most treasured "wisdom."

Actually the word "irritated" misrepresents what happens to me. In fact my life becomes disoriented; I respond with intransigence; I feel alienated from others, myself, even from God. This happens regardless of the countless times I promise God to remain open to new wisdom or petition God to open my eyes, my mind, and my heart. Fortunately God will not let me settle for the past. Instead God nudges, sometimes kicks, me into new situations in which the old proverbs serve as way stations to new discernment. But God appears in the new as well as the old. For the fear of God is the beginning of knowledge. Only fools despise such wisdom and learning.

How Do People Change?

Genesis 28:10-22, Hosea 2:2-15

Lord, how do people change?
    What makes us really different?

    We know people who take up new causes,
        Or adopt the language of a different group,
    Others who give up destructive habits,
        Or wear clothing that connects them with a new group.

    Some make sure their change is visible,
        Pressing their newness on us with insistent words.
    But so much remains the same,
        The attitude, the manner, and even the personality.

    It seems hopeless to expect a basic change;
        The world that formed us cannot be tossed aside.

Even so, Lord, help us to value changes that do take place,
    Not always overnight, but over a year, 3 years, or even 10:

    Mistakes we don't have to make again,
        because we suffered through them once;
    Ideas we have discovered
        that help us see the world differently;
    People we know
        who change us in ways we seldom notice;
    Memories we acquire,
        providing a reservoir of new possibilities.

Lord, be with those hardened against change,
    Those who build walls for protection
        Against the pain of shattered hopes,
            Against the agony of betrayed love,
        Against the fear of the unexpected,
            Against the terror of the unknown,
    Those who erect a fortress to protect
        Ideas that have worked in the past,
            Beliefs that were good enough for an earlier time,
        Feelings that must not be lost,
            Habits that have become precious.

Be with us when we change,
    And forgive us when we won't.

We pray in the name of the one
    who walks with us into each change,
        Jesus Christ our Lord   Amen.

The Beginning of Knowledge

Women and Men

Genesis 2:18-25, Galatians 3:23-29

God, creator of women and men,
　　placing two sexes on one planet has made for a lot of confusion,
　　　　a lot of excitement to be sure,
　　　　　　but a lot of confusion.

　Who belongs where?
　　　Are there any tasks save one
　　　　　that belong only to
　　　　　　　one sex or the other?

　Clearly we have divided up the activity
　　　more neatly than you intended
　　　　　With one sex providing bread and water
　　　　　　and the other cooking the food,
　　　　　With one sex watching the soaps
　　　　　　and the other glued to wrestling,
　　　　　With one sex unable to open the hood of a car
　　　　　　and the other oversudsing the washer.

God, it really is more confusing than our stereotypes
　　To allow people to have a fitting role in your world
　　　That works for their size and their sex,
　　　　Fits with their gifts and desires.

　Don't give up on us if we stay mixed-up for a long time,
　　　But don't let us get by with rejecting responsibility
　　　　because it's all confusing.

We pray in the name of the one
　　who chose only men as disciples
　　　　and spoke only to women at the tomb,
　　　　　Jesus Christ our Lord. Amen.

Unfinished

Exodus 23:12, Genesis 2:2-3

The moon was unfinished last night, God,
Just a sliver of what it takes to be full.

And so are we:
books to read,
sometimes boring;
reports to write,
often drudgery;
meals to prepare,
usually pedestrian;
sermons to preach,
mostly unspectacular;
rooms to clean,
whenever we get to it.

We look at your world, God,
And see a ton of things unfinished.
It makes us tired just looking,
Exhausted trying to decide where to begin.

Help us take a moment to rest, Lord,
Free us from constant focus on the undone and not right,
So that we might see what requires no work from us,
Good just as we have it now:

The leaf turning yellow,
The book already written,
The color of the evening sky,
The idea already passed on,
The path there for us to walk,
The melody already heard.

Thank you, God, for the finished parts of the world,
gifts that only ask us to receive,
places that simply want us to rest.

We pray in the name of the one
whose work did not prevent him from rest
around the table and beside the road,
Jesus Christ our Lord. Amen.

The Beginning of Knowledge

Snow Flurries

Luke 11:5-8, Luke 7:1-10

God, the forecaster said maybe snow flurries later,
    At least turning colder, much colder.

    How do the seasons and their weather affect us,
        Determining our actions, our feelings, maybe even
        thoughts?

    Some dread the coming winter,
        Depressed as the January thermometer.
            Our chill infects those around us.

    Some find their spirits soar with the snow,
        White flakes whirling out of the sky.
            Our smile thaws the frozen expression of others.

Grant us, Lord, a friend who sees the world differently than we,
    As irritating as that may be at times.

    Remind us that our thoughts, as wonderful as they may seem,
    Don't have the only claim on truth.

    Protect us from ascribing perfection to our feelings,
    Declaring as strange any deviation from our norm.

God, as we face winter,
    With anticipation or dread,
        Remind us of those who know not what they think and feel
            About winter or any season,
                Those with thoughts scrambled
                    by disease, injury, or drugs,
                Those with feelings damaged
                    by birth, exhaustion, or abuse.

    And whatever the weather, God,
        Don't let it stay too long;
            Someone doesn't like
                the current season.

We pray in the name of the one
    who walked through all the seasons of Galilee,
        Jesus Christ our Lord. Amen.

So Familiar

Deuteronomy 6:4-5,   Genesis 1:1

God, the text before us is so familiar,
    We can repeat it from memory,
        Some of us even in Hebrew.
    And yet we feel a bit cautious;
        The Bible's most familiar words can hide surprises.

Perhaps it is not so different with people, Lord.
    We talk to the same people everyday;
        We can almost pre-record their responses.
    We know what makes him anxious and angry;
        We remember what excites and energizes her.

    Thank you, God for familiar people,
        Even if they be weird or neurotic.
           We know the territory well.

And yet, God, in those people who are most familiar,
    There are parts that we have never seen.

    They can act in ways really bizarre.
        A selfish child may give away the largest cookie;
           A quiet adult may explode in anger.
        An impatient woman may take time to explain;
           An ordered man may lose control.

    Thank you, God, for the mysterious hidden in the familiar.
        Help us to run toward the new in our friends,
           Even when we preferred what we knew before.

We pray in the familiar name of the one from Nazareth
    who always brings surprises,
        Jesus Christ, our Lord. Amen.

Shadow of the Trees

God, the shadows of the trees have begun to change
    From the sharp outline of February
        Toward the full leafed shadow cast in May.

    We feel our spirits change as well:
        The moments of cold winter winds,
            The times of warm spring breeze,
        The moments of death and sterility,
            The occasions of new life and creativity.

God, be with those this day
    for whom spring seems never to come,
        The hate that sees only the outline of winter trees,
            The oppression that kills the buds before they
            burst,
        The fear that avoids all shadows,
            The grief that clouds the eye with tears.

God, help us to live out the spring
    when it comes,
        To hand a leaf to one who is lonely,
            To direct a gentle breeze toward an angry soul,
        To invite under your branches one who is afraid,
            To offer another way to one who destroys new life.

We pray in the name of the one
    through whom all new life comes,
        Jesus Christ our Lord. Amen.

Goodbye

Song of Songs 3:1-4, John 19:25-27

God, it is difficult to say, "Goodbye,"
   Unless we never said, "Hello."

   We see each other most every day:
      A recognizable voice, even over the phone,
      A familiar walk, even from a distance,
      An understandable opinion, even when wrong.

   The bond has been tested:
      Tears need not be hidden,
      Anger didn't drive us apart,
      Laughter could be spontaneous.

God, we don't know how the union grew:
   No one tried to make it happen.
      It came almost without notice,
         Comfort deepened in moments
            No one can recall.

   It seems better
      not to travel together
         If our roads must divide.
   It seems easier
     To go to new places
        If we left no friends behind.

But God, friendship does come,
   A gift from you,
      The gift of life.

   Be with the leaving and the left,
      The new beginnings that demand an end.
   Comfort us when we find only tears
      In the loss of separation.
   Provide for us new friends
      When life takes away the ones we love.

We pray in the name of the one
   who knew both leaving and being left,
      Jesus Christ our Lord. Amen.

The Chase

Ruth 4:13-17,   Luke 8:43-48

God, we chase your path to the future,
Hoping not to lose the way:

Down interstate highway,
And through dark alleys;
In quiet woods,
And up noisy streets;
In public meetings,
And behind closed doors;
At the desk,
And on the beach;
In the traffic,
And on the bed;
At the stove,
And behind the mower.

Sometimes the chase seems endless,
Even fruitless, God

Until a baby arrives
Or an old man rests;
Until a flower blooms
Or an idea dawns;
Until a body is healed
Or a soul calmed;
Until a weapon is tossed aside
And a new way found.

Give us strength to walk on,
And patience with those who tire.
Free us to celebrate even a moment's joy,
And to be gentle even with ourselves.

We pray in name of the patient one from Nazareth
who tirelessly walks before us,
Jesus Christ our Lord. Amen.

Comfort and Challenge

Matthew 11:28-30, Isaiah 43:18-19

God of comfort and care:
    As heat seems to come in unwanted amounts,
        Too much in August,
           Too little in February,
    So pain finds its way into every life,
        If not this day then the next:
        The loss of
           a loved one,
                a healthy body,
           a dream;
        The violation of
           a friendship,
                a personality,
           a covenant.

God of comfort and care:
    Lead us through the despair of loss.
        Calm the rage of violation
    So that we might laugh beyond despair,
        and love beyond rage.

God of challenge and change:
    As order seeks to absorb creativity,
        and tradition turns unexpectedly to stone,
    So I elevate my preferences to divine command,
        and my habits to natural law.
        My preference for
           a neat room to trashy,
                quiet music to lasting,
           Christian values to any other,
        My habit of
           running life on a careful schedule,
                living out middle American mores,
           evaluating a day according to its productivity.

God of challenge and change:
    Bend the track of our rut
        So that we can see the pilgrimage of a stranger.
    Grant us humility with our passion
        So that we can listen to the soul of one different.

We pray in the name of the prophet/priest from Galilee,
    Jesus Christ our Lord. Amen.

The Beginning of Knowledge

Winter Trees

Luke 2:40-52, John 3:1-8

It is beautiful, God,
    The winter tree in the winter sun,
        No straight lines
           Like people make;
        Branches reddened by the sun,
           Going every which way,
                Without organization,
                    But with no superficiality.

I want not to look like a winter tree, God,
    Going every which way,
        Without visible organization.

When I don't plan,
    It usually shows;
        Unlike your trees,
           It seldom looks beautiful.

Yet it is there, Lord,
    Hidden beneath the visible covering,
        The unplanned, every-which-way growth in me.

Help me enjoy the strength of that chaos
    That belongs only in your organization.
But don't leave me with only that, God,
    So that I can never plan any direction in my life.

And God, stay close to those who never notice a winter tree,
    Either before them or within.

We pray in the name of the tree of life,
    Jesus Christ our Lord. Amen.

Heard In Our Land

No Peace and Quiet

Focus text:

I have no peace;
I have no quiet;
I have no rest;
Trouble comes.

— Job 3:26

We demand peace and quiet, sometimes in fun, other times in irritation. Yet of course it can be more serious than that. Trouble that reaches into the soul disturbs all the elements that might provide peace and quiet. The dark of night becomes ominous rather than quieting. The bed becomes lumpy rather than soothing. Food becomes compulsive rather than satisfying. Friends become interruptive, rather than relaxing. Solitude becomes lonely rather than calming. Even the toilet becomes a problem rather than relieving. There is no peace, no quiet, no rest.

No biblical character understood that better than Job. Job's poetry exploded in anger toward other people and God. He languished in despair about his situation and his future. He pled that the pain of his present not go on forever. On the one hand Job trusted that if God only cared and would intervene then Job would have peace and quiet. On the other hand Job found God's visits only worsened his situation and increased his trauma. Even prayer which had before provided peace and quiet, now generated confusion and increased anger. Job's previous trust that God wills shalom for everyone created rage because there was no peace and quiet and rest anywhere, not even through prayer.

Of course Job is not the only biblical character to experience the hurt of violation in their faith pilgrimage. The anger that burst forth from Hannah because of her infertility frightened her husband and caused the priest Eli to assume that she was drunk or deranged. The shock of learning that the ark of the Lord had fallen into Philistine hands caused Eli to fall out his chair, fatally breaking his neck. Jesus was no stranger to hurt and anger on the way from the manger to the cross.

Pain invades the life of every individual, not just less fortunate people far away. However, we seem somewhat more reluctant than our biblical ancestors to include our personal hurt and anger in our prayers. We prefer to keep our petitions orderly and our address to God limited to praise. Are we less convinced than Job and Hannah that God wills good for our lives? Are we not willing to risk holding God partly responsible when the shalom can nowhere be found? Perhaps we fear that God cannot handle our anger or will be put off by it. Maybe we accept all the responsibility ourselves or blame other people or forces. I suspect, when it comes to prayer generated by anger, hurt, resentment and rage, we have much to learn from Sarah, Abraham, Hannah, David, Job and others.

Heard In Our Land

Not Just at the Edges

Genesis 3:16-19,   2 Corinthians 1:8-11

God, we see pain at the very center of life,
    Not just at the edges,
        Where we can put it out of sight,
            Building residences for painful people,
    Not just in a distant land,
        Where we can turn off the news,
            And demand that somebody do something to help.

No, God, we feel the pain in our own soul
    When we work so hard
        And no one notices,
    When we offer ourselves
        And there is no place we fit,
    When we look around
        And see the people we've hurt,
    When we make a mistake
        And people laugh,
    When we offer love
        And get back indifference,
    When we close our life
        And see we didn't matter.

Come, Lord, into our pain.
    Take away what can be removed,
        Protect us from complete destruction,
            Anesthetize us if you must.

Come, God, beyond our hurt,
    That in spite of our own pain
        Or because of it,
    We can feel the hurt of others,
        Our sister beside us,
            Our brother far away,
                Our cousin locked up.

We pray in the name of the one
    whose life mingled sorrow and love on a cross,
        Jesus Christ, our Lord. Amen.

General Hospital

Genesis 15:1-6, Psalm 13

God, your drama sometimes feels like daytime TV,
  General Hospital almost.
      Whatever we promise,
        We break.
      Whatever you promise,
        Waits until the next show.

God, of course it is supposed to be all our fault,
  And lots of times it is
      Like when we prefer cheap bananas for us
        To fair wages for the poor,
      Or use your name
        To earn money for a Mercedes,
      Or become a pastor
        So somebody will notice,
      Or point to the Bible
        So that we can win.
  Perhaps most of the time
      We break our promises
        And crucify you.

But God there are other times
  When we give ourselves in love
      And feel violated,
  When we give our energy to your realm
      And it doesn't matter,
  When we commit our life blood
      And end up written out of the script,

There are times when life is not fair,
  And it is not our fault.
      It's yours,
        If you care.
  We are supposed to understand,
      Or let it be your mystery.
  But your mystery hurts us,
      Like our betrayal
        Hurts you.

God, help us to be as willing to forgive you
  As we are eager to be forgiven,
      To understand you
        As we expect to be understood.
We pray in the name of the physician from Galilee,
      Jesus Christ our Lord. Amen.

Carried Alone

God, we know so little about each other.
What about the problems of those around us,
some, most perhaps, carried alone?

Sometimes it seems best to carry hurt alone,
Sharing the pain might injure another.
Indiscriminate disclosure generates catastrophe.

But the pain remains there, Lord:
a loved one lost,
a relationship betrayed,
separation,
violation,
illness of the body,
anguish in the soul,
perpetual pain,
spiritual sterility.

See it, God, between us and among us.
We need not hunt for the hurt ones;
We are they.

Touch each one,
Wherever the pain,
With a song from the soul,
A smile from a friend.

Even as we lift our pain to you, Lord,
What about all the hurt that events must bring you?
A world preoccupied with making love and war
and not sure which is which,
A world that rapes the land you give
and offers back waste,
A world that crucifies the one you sent
and hardly notices.

God, show us the way beyond our pain and yours.
Help laughter sneak through our sorrow and yours.
Let us find moments
When we can be your people
And you will be our God;
When no one studies war,
Even animals lie under the trees together;
When the tomb turns up empty
And we are all at rest,
through Jesus Christ our Lord. Amen.

No Peace and Quiet   79

Angry at Each Other

Genesis 4:1-16,   I Kings 1:41–2:25

Sisters and brothers angry at each other, God.
    It may not be anything important—except to them.

    Is the tension normal?
        It seems impossible to avoid.
    From where does it arise?
        It seems to just appear.
    How will end, Lord?
        Someone's likely to be destroyed

        by a hand gun we have a right to own,
            by a word which wounds the soul,
        by an explosion that irradiates the earth,
            by a whisper that ruins a life.

    Will it never end, God,
        Until everyone is destroyed?

        Perhaps you could remove the tension,
            Have life without occasion for anger.
        Would that be the good life?
            We seem unable to make much good
                Of life with strife.

    However undesirable, we may feel it,
        Life with tension appears to be our lot, God.

        Grant us the creativity to resolve conflict without
            destruction,
        And extend to us more compassion than we usually share
            with one another.

We pray in the name of the one
    who chose to be destroyed rather than to destroy,
        Jesus Christ our Lord. Amen.

Full of Vengeance

Genesis 4:17-26,   Matthew 18:23-35

The world is full of vengeance, God.
    Revenge exists within us, around us, against us.

    We know about the desire to get even.
        The darkness comes when we've been violated,
            Deep and raging,
                Intense and frightening.

    We can handle it most of the time,
        Confine it to our daydreams,
            Share it with a friend,
                Let go soon enough.

    Revenge gets away from us once in a while,
        Pops out against people
            Or places it doesn't belong.
    God, even if we control the expression of our own revenge,
        We have no control over others.
            Seventy have been killed for a slight,
                Or worse, much worse.

Thank you, God, for people who listen to the heart,
    Helping release others' revenge in acceptable ways.

    Thank you God, for saints,
        People who don't act out the vengeance they feel.

        Thank you God, for worship,
    A chance to face our darkness and receive a new start.

    Thank you God, for a future,
One beyond revenge, violence, and destruction.

We pray in the name of the pioneer of that future
    just three days beyond revenge,
        Jesus Christ our Lord. Amen.

No Peace and Quiet

Families

Genesis 9:20-27, Mark 3:31-35

God, families are odd groups.
    Mostly we didn't choose each other.
        Usually we learn to get along
            In some fashion or other.

    We learn each other's habits:
        What she looks like in the morning,
            What he sounds like in the shower,
        How she wants her eggs,
            What he won't eat at all.

    We learn what hurts the other:
        How to bruise her ego,
            How to wound his vanity,
        How to agitate her rage,
            How to make him feel ashamed.

Thank you, God, for the family that nurtured us.
    Well, thanks for some things they did,
        But other parts hurt,
            And the memory still does.

    Sometimes the family took how they knew us,
        And used it against us,
            Once in while in jest,
                Occasionally for profit.

    Help us, God, find ways beyond those painful memories,
        To hand them to history, even when we visit.
    We can't hide the scars, Lord,
        But keep us from always pointing to them.

We pray in the name of the one
    who had a family too,
        Jesus Christ our Lord. Amen.

You Remain Silent

Ruth 1:1-5, Genesis 43:1-14

God, what are we to do
As we stand in a swirl of confusing events,
Losing our way to the future,
And you remain silent?

A husband dies—a wife left empty,
A daughter killed—parents filled with rage,
A famine strikes—refugees crowd the road,
A river floods—cots fill the gym.

Where are you, God,
When disaster strikes,
And you remain silent?

Many say, "We need only listen.
God always speaks.
We seldom listen."

You know that's not true, God,
Sometimes, perhaps, but not always.
We listen hard,
And hear only silence.
The silence sounds deafening
To those who seek to follow.

God, we do not know what happens
That we must act,
And you are silent.

Forgive us when we act
Out of your silence,
And bring sickness,
Instead of health.

We pray on behalf of the widows, the orphans, the aliens,
In the name of the one who knew the silence of the cross,
Jesus Christ our Lord. Amen.

No Peace and Quiet

A Chance to Fail

Job 1–2, Matthew 5:13

God, lead us not into temptation;
　　Deliver us from the test.

　A test comes to us, Lord, as a threat,
　　A chance to fail.

　　　We can find no hiding place from a failed test,
　　　　Exposed —not good enough;
　　　The test that comes from you
　　　　Shames to the very depth our soul.

　Remember, God, the petition Jesus taught us to pray:
　　Lead us not into the test,
　　　Deliver us from evil.

Tests do come, Lord,
　　Sometimes, apparently, with your permission.
　　　And we do fail,
　　　　And we are ashamed or angry,
　　　　　And we hide and deny,
　　　　Or we confess and hope for the best.

　Thank you, God, when we find ourselves embraced,
　　Loved on the other side of a failed test:
　　　The arms of a friend
　　　　to break the fall,
　　　A new dream
　　　　in the terror of the night,
　　　A warm breeze
　　　　on a frozen soul.

We pray in the name of the one
　　who passed his test and ours,
　　　Jesus Christ our Lord. Amen.

Love Troubles Me

Mark 12:31, Matthew 5:43-48

Love troubles me, God.

It involves my feelings of affection for others.

Most feelings of love fit the situation,
Love for my family and friends.
Of course I get angry too.
Then I don't feel much affection.

But some affection goes in odd directions,
People near or far who I barely know.
Those feelings are often misunderstood
By others and by me.

Love is not just my feelings, God.

It involves my actions.

Mostly I want to help people near and far
Find their way to a full life,
Teach them what I know,
Share with them my soul.

But sometimes I want to hurt others,
Pay them back for humiliating me,
Plot revenge for injustice,
Satisfy the rage churning in me.

Thanks, God, for the love that abides in me,
The joy I find in affection and assistance.

Care for the times I can't or won't love, God.
Help me turn my drive for vengeance over to you.
In the name of the lover and loved one from Nazareth,
Jesus Christ our Lord. Amen.

Enemies

Job 29–30, Matthew 5:11-12

I have enemies, God:
    Some of them are active and personal,
        People who have violated me,
            Others who wish me ill health.
    Some enemies are corporate, even impersonal,
        People whose actions endanger our present or future,
            Others who seek to destroy what I know to be true.

What can I do about them, God?
    My emotions don't respond to an internal directive,
        Ordering me to feel kindly toward them.
    My commitment won't allow me vindictiveness.
        Besides, I wouldn't feel better.

Many sermons would order me to love,
    Act differently than I feel.
        I suppose I could do that,
    But I would be split,
        Divided against myself.

Perhaps, God, you could find a way through.
        Help, me step back and watch,
            Wait, and listen as deeply as I can.
        Maybe then, I could act with integrity
            In ways that will heal instead of hurt
                Me or them.

But if not,
    If I must always live with this pain,
        Give me other chances to act
            And to love with integrity
                Even those I might call "enemy."

    We pray in the name of the friend from Nazareth,
        Jesus Christ our Lord. Amen.

Extending a Hand

Focus text:

She extends her hand to the poor,
She opens her arms to those who need help.

— **Proverbs 31:20**

In Proverbs 31, a sage in ancient Israel describes the ideal woman in terms of her character and behavior. While many would wish to add some elements and subtract others to the description in Proverbs, few in the community of faith would leave out verse twenty from the description of the "ideal" woman or man. Helping, serving, caring have marked the central thrust of all ministry grounded in the Bible. In fact while the noun "minister" denotes an ecclesiastical office, the verb, "to minister" refers to an act of extending a hand to those who need help.

Perhaps because it is such a central element in the community of faith, the helping ministry becomes as much a bone of contention as a centering symbol. Did I really help the person? I never seem to know. What starts out helping sometimes ends up causing more problems than originally existed. There is always some other "minister" who feels that I have misunderstood what assistance was needed. But then he or she discovers the same problem when they try to extend a helping hand. Must I always help? I often find myself intimidated by the parable of the "Good Samaritan" (Luke 10:29-37). I am worried that I will be one of those that "pass by on the other side." I know I cannot minister to every needy situation. I have neither the skill nor the energy. Yet the ideal Christian is always pictured with extended hands and open arms. It is an exhausting picture.

Perhaps others are able to sort out all this service responsibility better than I can. But service is so central to my understanding of Jesus that I will probably remain confused for some time to come. I am afraid of looking, let alone being, "anti-service," lest in my own eyes I land on the "left hand" in the parable of the last judgment (Matt. 25:31-46), regardless of how God evaluates the situation.

Really, of course, fear of being a "leftist" in terms of the last judgment is not my motivation as much as a deep sense that the ancient sage is correct. The model person (hence "faithful Christian") always extends a hand to the poor and approaches those who need help with open arms. Therefore I suspect that as I work with biblical texts focused on service, the prayers that come to my lips will always express a certain amount of confusion and frustration.

Fragile Commodity

Luke 10:29-37, 2 Kings 5:1-27

God, care seems such a fragile commodity in the world
    threatened by compulsive care-givers and chronic indifference.

    Sometimes we can find only bad Samaritans,
        People who rush around hunting for others lying
            at the side of the road,
        Descending on
            Anything that might need care,
                However remotely.

    Lord, keep our care tuned to the others' needs,
        Addressing wisely and genuinely the crises around us.

God, at times we can find no Samaritans anywhere,
    Only injured people lying beside the road
        Amid the wrecked automobiles
            and rusted guns,
        Between the broken relationships
            and shattered dreams.

    Lord, turn aside those still on their feet
        at least some of the time.
            Raise up daughters and sons willing and
                able to make life happen.

    And God, help us all,
        the care-givers and cared-for,
            to trust the life you bring
                through Jesus Christ our Lord. Amen.

Forever Around

Ruth 2:1-23, Leviticus 19:9-10

God, we have another problem,
    Actually the same one:
        Those who can't feed, clothe and house themselves.
        They seem to be forever around.

    We try all kinds of programs:
        Grain that is left behind,
            Cheese that isn't sold,
        Fallow fields,
            Food pantries,
        Jubilee years,
            Food stamps.

    But the people are still there,
        Not mean people.
            Well some are,
                The ones that make headlines.
    But most are O.K. folk
        With little to eat,
            No place to sleep,
                Tattered clothes.

God, we want to quit,
    Retire to deep thoughts and flowery prayers,

    Until health bankrupts our parents,
        Farm prices displace our sister,
            Cheap imports lay off our friend.

Help us to remember, God,
    Not everyone has a child, a sister or a friend
        To cushion their failure
            With a meal, a hug, and a bed.

But accept us, God,
    When our giver runs dry,
        And our helper stops up,
            while still there remains
                the hungry, homeless, and lonely.

We pray in the name of the one
    who calls us to serve,
        knowing the weariness of lots of people and little food,
        Jesus Christ our Lord. Amen.

No One Noticed

Genesis 24:1-67,   Romans 16:1-16

God, so much happens to us that we never remember,
Events in our lives that we never notice:

    A brother helps smooth out a quarrel,
      No one remembers;
    A sister decides not to retaliate for an insult,
      No one noticed;
    A teacher helps us really understand,
      No one remembers;
    A student quietly softens a teacher's hurt,
      No one noticed;
    A child sits patiently while adults talk,
      No one remembers;
    An adult picks up a fallen child,
      No one noticed.

Lord, there is so much we might have learned
    from what we don't remember.
Relationships would have been so much different if we had noticed.

    Comfort, Lord, the servant whose work no one remembers.
    Publicize the one whose actions no one noticed.

    Teach us, Lord, to watch more closely as life goes by.
      Forgive us for the gifts we lose
        Because of
          Memory loss and
          Myopic vision.

We pray in the name of the one
    almost no one noticed until he was gone,
      Jesus Christ our Lord. Amen.

Passion for Justice

Genesis 34:1-31, Psalm 72:1-4

God, you hear the cries of the oppressed and give them life.
    You pursue justice to the ends of the earth.

        Our passion for justice seldom matches yours.
            Even our most fervent efforts fall short.

        Indeed, God, sometimes it feels like simple justice is not
enough.
            Justice slips away when we try to create it.

            Are the large corporations callous and uncaring,
                Or are the workers self-centered and greedy?

            Is the parent autocratic and irritable,
                Or are the kids demanding and lazy?

            Is the dictator exploitive and repressive,
                Or are freedom fighters violent and power hungry?

            Is the teacher narrow and unreasonable,
                Or are the students rebellious and cynical?

Forgive us, Lord, when we race in waving the flag of justice
    Only to confuse the situation, making it worse.

        But help us not to give up on justice
            when situations seem to defy solution.

        Strengthen our resolve to listen for justice
            when our best efforts go awry.

        Reduce our anxiety about justice
            when circumstances require generations to renew.

We pray in the name of the one
    who never found justice simple yet never gave up,
        not even today,
            Jesus Christ our Lord. Amen.

We Need Help

Mark 10:13-16, Mark 3:1-6

God, how do we get people to care,
to give themselves to life when death seems to control.

Your world needs people willing to make life happen;
We find ourselves surrounded by those who stare at death:

Death from misfortune, illness or accident,
things over which they have no control;
Death from bad choices,
choices which they wish they could undo;
Death from technology,
technology which outruns our ability to cope.

How do we get people to see,
to be willing to respond as they must?

We want to shake them and make them,
scream at them and force them.
"Act for goodness sake!"
"Help bring life!"

Yet, Lord, we don't want a world of shaking and making,
people who assist because they are forced.

We need help,
but help that comes by choice.
We need love,
but love that is genuinely given,
Help and love, not just for ourselves,
but for each individual
and all of us together.

God, make us bringers of life,
and help us trust the life you bring
through Jesus Christ our Lord. Amen

Duty Decides

Joshua 2:1-21,   I Samuel 25:1-42

God, what does love mean in a world where duty decides,
Where obedience and responsibility are the important words?

Can compassion be more than a hope
that acts around the edges when duty isn't looking?
Can love be more than a dream
that looks with a frown at a world run by requirements?

God, love and compassion seem soft
in a tough world,
and we need soft spots.
But how much do they matter?

Computers do not run on compassion.
The stock market does not function on care.
Soccer must be played by certain rules.
Science depends on method.

And yet, Lord, it is not quite enough
to leave love and compassion as second class.

Limits build distance.
Duty dulls enthusiasm.
Requirements create antagonism.
Obedience seldom cares.

If not for compassion, obedience hardens and breaks apart;
except for love, duty cracks and tumbles down.

Ah, God, it is not easy to sort out,
Often more difficult to live.

Help us Lord, discern when to say, "will you?"
and when to declare, "you will!"
and how to say them both at the same time
as you did in Jesus Christ our Lord. Amen.

Always More To Do

Genesis 2:2-3,   Isaiah 32:14-18

God, the world seems never at rest.
    Nothing ever feels finished,
        Always more to do.

    We look at a world of evil empires
        and unmown grass;
    We peer into a reflection of incompetence
        and uncombed hair.

Except the work does not fall equally on all people.
    Some people do almost nothing,
        Except watch the perpetual movement on the TV screen,
    Where folk never go to bed to sleep,
        And bathrooms need not function as designed.

Give rest to your world, God,
    to the terrorist who longs to end oppression,
        to the domestic who awakes each morning to a dirty house,
    to the president who wants to make the world safe,
        to the unemployed who greets each day from the same chair;

    to the student who rushes from class to class,
        to the comatose who lies motionless,
    to the industrialist who sees the future in charts,
        to the lover who waits long hours for a moment.

Give rest to your world, God,
    Through the quiet one from Galilee,
        Jesus Christ our Lord, Amen.

A Friend

Job 2:11-13, 1 Samuel 20:1-42

God, how can I be a friend?
    What kind of friend do I need?
        Who do I want as friend?

Wants are easiest for me to identify, God.
    Usually I want a friend who will agree with me,
        Tell me that I am right,
            Regardless of the truth.

    Sometimes friends tell me that they understand,
        Except there always seems to be a "but":
           "But" they don't agree;
               "But" they see the other side.
        Mostly I don't want "buts,"
          I want allies,

Except, God, when friends sacrifice their integrity
    Just to stay friends with me.
        Later I may need their honesty.
           Dishonest allies make poor friends.

What do I need in a friend, Lord?
    Sometimes gentle, sometimes powerful;
        Sometimes agreement, sometimes challenge;
    Sometimes lover, sometimes thinker.
        Usually I need a friend a lot more
            perceptive,
                astute,
                    careful
    Than I.

God, grant to everyone a friend,
    The sort they need, maybe even want,
        One modelled on our Friend from Nazareth,
        Jesus Christ our Lord. Amen.

Arguments

Job 4–5, John 3:1-21

God, we don't belong in these arguments,
    Trying to badger people into hope:

    The 5'4", 125 pound teenage girl,
        that she is not dumb, fat, and ugly;
    The 90 year old grandmother,
        that the family does want her at Christmas;
    The abandoned wife,
        that she can make it on her own;
    The nonathletic junior high boy,
        that *nerd* and *wimp* do not measure his worth;
    The suddenly blind,
        that physical disability does not destroy life;
    The daughter of divorcing parents,
        that she did not cause and cannot stop the separation.

God, we are taught not to try to persuade,
    Just listen and reflect feelings.

        Stay with us, God.
            We want to say more than:
                "I sense you are hurt,"
                    "That makes you angry,"
                "You seem to be lonely."
        Those words sound phony after awhile.
        So we say the wrong thing
            And end up arguing with a person
            Already hurt and angry.

Help us find new ways to be a friend.
    Most of all,
        Don't let us stop trying,
            In the name of Jesus Christ our Lord. Amen.

Sojourners

Genesis 12:10-20, Luke 9:57-62

God, the world seems crowded with sojourners,
  Folk driven into a foreign land by chance, circumstances or choice.
    Some have been forced from home by famine,
      Forced to live each day dependant on the local
      citizens for food.
    Others have been driven into exile by power or conscience,
      Forced to find work in a land that doesn't care
      about their skills.
    Some have chosen to follow their dreams to a new country,
      Required to rebuild their life in a land that can't
      understand their speech.

Lord, the world seems crowded with sojourners,
  Folk who find themselves with no safe place even in their
  homeland,
    Those whose homes were dissolved by the choice of another,
      Their safe place replaced by shattered hopes and
      crushed dreams,
    Those with people around and no one to trust,
      None they can allow to enter their soul,
    Those who choose what seems half a home,
      And drown their loneliness in activity or alcohol.

God, who blesses the alien and sojourner,
  Touch with your rest
    the confused, the dependant, and the isolated.
  Speak to the heart of
    the left, the lost, and the lonely.

Remind us all of the sojourner from Galilee,
  who had no place to lay his head,
    yet never found himself cut off from your home,
    Jesus Christ our Lord. Amen.

Heard In Our Land

Special Times

Focus text:
These are the special times of the Lord, holy gatherings, to which you shall summon them in the appointed season.
— Leviticus 23:4

The community of faith has always had special times throughout the year, times when we stop doing the ordinary things and remember to attend to the extra-ordinary. Among the special times in ancient Israel, four became especially prominent: Passover and Unleavened Bread, which focused especially on the story of the Exodus; the Feast of Weeks or Pentecost, which marked the spring grain harvest and rehearsed the covenant at Sinai; the Festival of Booths, a time of thanksgiving for the harvest; and, in later Jewish history, the Day of Atonement, a time of confession and reconciliation with God. Of course other annual holidays emerged in addition to the weekly Sabbath.

Obviously, the Christian year revolves around Christmas and Easter, the "extra" special times of the church year. As with most of the festivals in ancient Israel these two holy days have elements that focus on religious remembering and other elements related more to the rhythm of the life of the people. In the United States, Christmas extends all the way from the harvest festival of Thanksgiving at the end of November through New Year's Day on January first. Easter marks not only the death and resurrection of Jesus, but also the beginning of Spring.

Christmas and Easter are occasions of great joy and that joy erupts in song and prayer. But the joy of the sacred tradition sometimes buries other feelings that accompany these two great sacred festivals. One supposes God understands that around the edges of these special times, less visible events occur and invisible feelings appear. Those too invade our prayers, perhaps not in the authorized prayers of the seasons, but in the prayer life of the faithful.

The prayers in this chapter differ in origin from the others. They grew more out of the "special times," principally, but not exclusively Christmas and Easter, rather than study of particular biblical texts. For Christmas and Easter the biblical texts are well-known. For the other special times included in this chapter, the event and not a text prompted the prayer.

Holiday Offers

God, the newspaper bulges with holiday offers,
    TV ads display the magic of new products:

    A doll that replies to a child's voice,
        A stereo that reproduces sound more perfect than a concert
        hall,
    A macho robot that destroys evil toys,
        A food processor that creams carrots and fingers.

Thank you, God, for ingenuity and industry,
    For abundance and availability.

But God, hidden between ads for
    New model clothes and sexy cars,
        Fantasy cologne and seductive diapers,
    We find stories about death,
        on a distant sea,
            on a barren hillside,
        in a tropical village,
            on a city sidewalk.

Help us employ as much ingenuity and industry
    to quiet anger as to make new toys,
        to relax oppression as to computerize cars.

We pray in the name of the one
    who managed childhood without Mattel or Fisher Price,
        Jesus Christ our Lord. Amen.

— Christmas Season

Singing Angels and Somber Stable

We live in an interesting world, God:

> Warm reds and excited yellows light the holiday home,
> And sterile white and ominous black engulf illness and
> death;

> Tiny lights illuminate brightly decorated firs,
> And a stark outline of a winter maple arrests the eye;

> Quiet candles and energetic singing fill the church,
> And lonely silence crowds a single room;

> The taste of warm cut-out cookies and chocolate fudge push down
> on the scales,
> And the flavor of a cold hamburger salvaged from the trash
> numbs the hunger.

Thank you, God, for laughter and love,
> for presents and companionship,
For a new sweater that warms the body,
> For a stuffed animal that cuddles the imagination,
For a football that aches the muscles,
> For a book that gives wings to the soul.

Work together with us, God,
> To warm the unsweatered,
> > To cuddle the unloved,
> To exercise the unmoving,
> > To stimulate the unimaginative.

We pray in the name of the one
> born in the midst of the singing angels and somber stable,
> > Jesus Christ our Lord. Amen.

— Christmas Season

A Family Time

God, Christmas is a family time:
    Cousins who see each other only once a year,
        Sisters and brothers who bring a life time of memories,
    In-laws who may never have met,
        Parents who live for the time when everyone comes home.

Be with our family time, God:
    Help us remember what to say and what to avoid saying,
        Allow adults to be as excited about receiving as giving,
            Maybe even help a child be as excited about giving
            as receiving.

God, Christmas is a lonely time:
    Elderly who wait in vain for someone to visit,
        Internationals who spend the season in a new land with
        strange customs,
    Parents whose children are too scattered,
        The ill who feel only pain.

Be with the lonely, God:
    Slip through the coldness of their day
        Give them more for Christmas than another television
    program.
        Help us to see the lonely in our midst.

We pray in the name of the child
    born in a lonely stable that we might always have family,
        Jesus Christ our Lord. Amen.

— Christmas Season

Christmas Gifts

God, sometimes Christmas gifts just don't work.
 The heart is right; the gift all wrong.

 We anticipate the usual problems, Lord:
  Already three white shirts with a light blue pin stripe;
   Four long sleeved, white blouses with a bow at the
   collar.

 Apparently stores expect teenagers to return all gifts.
  Might as well hand them out on consignment,
   Jeans with just the right amount of stone washing,
    Sweaters exactly positioned between too gaudy
    and too plain.
  These nuances elude parental eyes.

 But, God, there is still another problematic group,
  Gifts like new vacuum sweepers, electric skillets and
  bifocal glasses,
   Gifts for jobs I don't want to do,
    Ages I don't want to be.

Still, God, thank you
 for the sound of children saying,
  "It's beautiful, Mom, but could I check about another
  color?"
   "It's just right, Dad, except I haven't been that
   small in four years."

Thank you, Lord,
 For ingenuity that enables aging eyes to see,
  For floors that need to be swept,
   For food that needs to be cooked.

Most of all, thank you God, for caring enough
 to send the very best,
  Jesus Christ our Lord. Amen.

— Christmas

A Moment of Peace

Thank you, God, for a moment of peace
    in the midst of an envelope of turmoil,
        for a touch of calm
            in the prevailing chaos:

    a time to laugh
        at our ability to generate activity,
    a time to relax
        when much remains undone,
    a time to daydream
        when others demand our attention,
    a time to talk
        about nothing in particular.

Thank you, Lord, for quiet and calm,
    for gentleness and silence.

We remember times when we could not be touched by quiet,
    when life seemed endless noise, internal and external:

    the noise of our own speech,
        the twisting of our stomach,
    the frenzy of our activity,
        the headache from our tension.

Perhaps that turmoil is upon us now;
    Certainly it will happen again, soon.

God, stay with others and with us
    when we work frantically to quiet our lives.
        Don't give us over to the blood pressure
        We seem intent on reaching.

Touch us now with your silence,
    The quiet calm of the Galilean,
        Jesus Christ, our Lord. Amen.

                    — Between Christmas and New Year

Birthday of a King

God, we are celebrating a birthday today,
The birthday of a King:

Not an ordinary "king" who sat on a throne,
But a King who walked the streets;
Not a king who ruled with power,
But a King who dreamed of a peace filled world;
Not a king with a royal name,
But a King named for a religious rebel.

As we remember Martin Luther King, Jr., God,
we hear again the dream you ignited in him.
And we confess that our dreams often turn to nightmares,
For they feature us in the center.

Give us the courage to follow your dream,
That all your children might be free,
Free in a way none of us can yet imagine,
Free to love one another with purpose,
Free to live for others with passion,
Free to know you as God.

We pray in the name of the one
in whom your dream seemed shattered,
only to rise again on the third day,
Jesus Christ our Lord. Amen.

— Martin Luther King, Jr. Day

The Cross

God, the cross belongs to this season of our year,
　　But we confess that we do not really understand the cross.

　　Kings we understand, whether ceremonial or real,
　　　　But not a king who dies on a cross.
　　If we really feel the cross,
　　　　it brings more pain than we can handle.
　　If we domesticate the cross,
　　　　it becomes an ornament that doesn't matter.

God, can you make meaning out of our confusion?
　　Can you create faithfulness out of our hesitancy?

　　We remember just now,
　　　　those too sad to think about kings and crosses;
　　　　　　for them pain is the only life they know.
　　　　　　　　Come gently into their hurt, Lord.
　　We also remember
　　　　those too concerned with royal power
　　　　　　to imagine how the cross might fit.
　　　　　　　　Come powerfully into their grandeur.

We pray in the name of the royal criminal from Galilee,
　　Jesus Christ our Lord. Amen.

　　　　　　　　　　　　　　　　　　— Easter

Spring

God, we have stumbled through winter;
>   Hopefully a revisit of winter is a long way off.
>>   A holiday came and went so fast we almost missed it;
>>>   Hopefully another one will happen soon.
>   Thank you for spring.
>>   It came just in time.
>>>   Please give us time to enjoy it.

It is fun, God,
>   Spring and holidays,
>>   And even winter,
>>>   At least when it is past.

We remember just now those who cannot say,
>   "It is fun,"
>>   Those for whom this holiday seemed just like the last,
>>>   Those who can't open their windows and let the wind warm their soul,
>>   Those for whom the Spring rain can't wash away their winter,
>>>   Those who unlike the robin, can't return home and no home comes to them.

>   We are some of those people,
>>   Unmoved,
>>>   Or unwarmed,
>>   Or unwashed,
>>>   Or unloved.

God, Help us to smell new life in the flower,
>   Touch the new life in the grass

But if that cannot happen, Lord,
>   Do not abandon us to television reruns,
>>   Alone, passive, glassy-eyed and bored.
>>>   Help us to celebrate the April in another's life
>>>>   Even if it is still February in our own.

We pray in the name of the one
>   through whom each new spring comes,
>>   Jesus Christ our Lord. Amen.

— Easter Vacation

Exciting and Dangerous

God, dedicating individuals to ministry
    feels both exciting and dangerous.

    Exciting to send them out,
        But into a dangerous world
            to reach beyond the mechanized morass
                and call forth the soul of a people,
            to slip through the teeming throngs
                and touch the lonely woman,
            to wander through the violent community
                and quiet the enraged man,
            to walk through the exploitive culture
                and heal the injured child.
        All of this in your name,
            With you at their side.

God, give them faith and hope, love and laughter,
    Faith enough to walk through the darkest valleys,
        Hope sufficient to go on through failure,
    Love enough to convert hatred,
        Laughter sufficient to transform tears.

And God, when their faith and laughter give out,
    hope and love expire,
        Speak sternly if you must,
            But forgive their misstep.
        Show them another day as you can,
            And carry them in your arms.

We pray in the name of the pastor from Nazareth,
    Jesus Christ our Lord. Amen.

                    — Dedication to Ministry

Symbols of the Faith

God, sometimes I wonder about the symbols of the faith.
　　There have not been many new possibilities considered.
　　　　We find ourselves depending on ones several centuries old.

Take bread for instance.
　　We haven't even made use of some of the fast food
　　varieties.
　　　　The authorized versions look like
　　　　　　they have been sold by the ream,
　　　　　　　　or stepped on with a golf shoe.

In addition, take the wine.
　　Actually you will have to, God,
　　　　My tradition isn't into wine.

And there's the rainbow.
　　That's a good one, I guess,
　　　　But you always position it behind telephone wires,
　　　　　　where I can't get a good picture.

God, how about ice cream as a symbol?
　　It could help us remember that Jesus remained cool in tense
　　situations.
　　　　We should use gourmet ice cream to be up to date.
　　　　　　The Scandinavian sounding kind from Hackensack, NJ.

Or maybe you could try popcorn.
　　That explodes with flavor when warmed by the Spirit.
　　　　It too comes in a gourmet variety.

Aerial firecrackers might be a possibility.
　　We could play hymn tunes in the sky.
　　　　They come in a rainbow of colors.

I guess, God, that would make the faith modern,
　　But probably tie it to my time and place.
　　　　Thank you for the symbols we have.
　　　　　　Help us to use them to remember you,
　　　　　　　　Even as they help you remember us.

We pray in the name of the one
　　who probably never tasted a gourmet anything,
　　　　Jesus Christ our Lord. Amen.

—— Communion